How To Write Any High School Essay

THE ESSENTIAL GUIDE

Jesse Liebman

FIRST EDITION

How To Write Any High School Essay:
The Essential Guide

Copyright © 2017 by Jesse Liebman

First Edition March 2017

Cover Design by Janine Agro

Author photograph by Lois Greenfield

ISBN: 978-1-53902-981-6

10 9 8 7 6 5 4 3 2 1

Printed in the United States of America

For my first teacher, my father:

A keen mind, a kind heart

TABLE OF CONTENTS

Summary of Quick Tips

INTRODUCTION

High school English, History, and Social Studies classes are generally considered to be the courses in which teenagers learn "how to write." By reading historical accounts and the exemplary literature of (mainly) the Western Tradition, it is presumed, the student becomes responsive to wonderful characters and cultures and learns how to critically appreciate many styles of prose writing. More generally, such courses seek to encourage students to understand the meaning of the Liberal Arts, the foundation of a lifetime of humanistic engagement with cultural experience. Beyond the middle school terminology, however—topic sentence, thesis statement, transition sentence—no formal advancement in writing technique is ever explicitly taught. By the time they reach high school, students are already supposed to know "how" to write. The result is a kind of frustrating chaos—both for the students who don't know what to do and for the teachers who must read and grade these "essays." This raises the important question: how *is* the high schooler supposed to learn how to write an excellent high school essay?

What is Writing?

Over the course of more than a decade tutoring young people attending both public and private schools in New York City, I've encountered many different kinds of students. Some read very well, but don't know how to write. Some are facile with the challenges of writing, but don't know how to read actively looking for detail. Some can express their thoughts well orally, but don't know how to make them come alive on the page. Some respond to comedy, but not tragedy. Some love war stories; others, love stories.

Before I begin working on writing with them, I always ask the same question: "What is writing?" I have elements of an answer in mind—answers that I've developed over the years—but I'm most interested in what *they* think writing is. I get wildly different answers. The best response I ever received, however, was from a student who said, quite honestly, "writing is work." Then he paused, and added: "Writing is a work of art." Yes, I thought. Both of those are true. Writing is work—hard work. And when a good writer does the hard work of writing, he or she can produce an elegant essay that conveys his or her thoughts in a persuasive, artful way. High school essays don't need to reach those ecstatic heights, but why not aim high?

The Essay

The word "essay" comes from the French verb "essayer," which means "to try, to attempt." The French word comes from the Latin verb "exigere," meaning "to ascertain, to weigh." Thus, in English, it's best to think of an essay as "a formal attempt to understand and evaluate something." The ideas I propose in this book follow from this understanding of what an essay is.

The High School Essay is not a College Essay

High school essays and college essays are very different creatures. College essays usually cover a wide range of material, whereas high school essays focus on, at most, one or two texts. Therefore, the limited focus of a high school essay is what's most important here. High school students are most often asked to dig into one specific text, to delve more deeply into a writer's world. In your high school essay, you are attempting to show how your understanding of a piece of literature (or a poem or an historical era) is accurate, concise, and supported sufficiently by evidence. College students are asked to do that *and* to discuss the bigger, broader sweep of literature, or of the writer's entire corpus, or of an entire historical era. As a result, college students have to do a lot of additional reading and research. These larger concerns, however, are not important in a high school curriculum. In addition, college professors often leave it up to students to choose their own essay topics, whereas high school teachers often prescribe formulaic questions. For all these reasons, what follows is targeted at high schoolers who are asked to write high school essays, responding to focused questions which require analyzing limited amounts of material in conventional ways.

This Book

This book is not a cheat sheet for your next essay on *Hamlet*. It will not necessarily help you get a good score on the essay section of the SAT.

Instead, this book is intended to give the high school student both a clear focus and an extra set of skills to use and adapt for his or her specific needs. Through simplification and choice of specific examples, it is intended to be a helpful guide for any essay the student may wish to write.

For those students with limited experience writing essays, this book will move through the entire writing process. For students already familiar with the big ideas of essay-writing, this book offers many time-saving and original ideas to help you make a strong impression on your teacher.

Take these ideas and make them your own. Use them as guideposts, strong enough to point in the right direction without necessarily mandating any specific path.

You and Your Teacher

Good teachers are your best friends. Bad teachers are your worst enemies. In either case, it is your teacher who grades your essays and your tests, and it is your teacher who has the final word. If anything in this book contradicts your teacher's explicit instructions, you should, no matter what, always follow what your teacher says (even if he or she is completely wrong).

CHAPTER 1

The Writing Process

Writing is a Process that Makes Thoughts Clear

Writing is a **process** that makes **thoughts** clear. Let me say it again in a slightly different way: Writing is a process through which **you** make **your thoughts** clear.

Let's start with **thoughts**. Thoughts are things that happen in your head. They sometimes take the form of ideas and at other times they are hunches, inklings, fancies, notions, and reactions. Thoughts sometimes are also arguments, sometimes opinions. They can also be called musings, explanations, and can convey strong feelings. Yes, a thought can convey feeling. Sometimes, your thoughts are excellent, imaginative, ground-breaking. At other times, they are boring, repetitive, insignificant. In order to write a thought, you must first *have* a thought. I encourage you to have as many thoughts as possible.

And now **process.** Writing is a process, which means it has a **beginning**, a **middle**, and an **end**. It is not one moment in time, nor one fixed thing. It requires a number of steps. Where to begin the process of writing? Why, at the beginning.

The Beginning of the Writing Process

At the **beginning** of the writing process are three essential steps: **reading**, **taking notes**, and **coming up with a question**.

1. Reading

Good writing begins with **good reading**. In the best of all possible worlds, you will have read every word that has been assigned to you by your teacher before you begin to think about writing your essay.

To write the best essay you can, you must spend time experiencing the world that the author has created—probing it, analyzing it, questioning it, making connections, making your reading personal. You don't have to like what you read. In fact, hating it is just as important, because that is your visceral reaction to the material, and your dislike could be the beginning of an original essay—filled with your perspective on why the book should be thrown in the garbage (or at least removed from high school curricula). But love or hate the book, you must still do so *specifically*: admire one character, revile another; enjoy one chapter, dislike another; praise the beginning, savage the ending; like one word, hate the next. These emotional reactions to a book can be the start of some excellent **thoughts**. They are essential to good reading.

Significance

As you read, you are looking for what is **significant**. Books can be long, and not every moment in them is so important or revealing. What you're looking for are those little gems of significance, those telling details that shape a deeper understanding of the author's world. You'll be able to find what is significant by looking for changes in three areas of significance: **Character**, **Relationship**, and **Plot**.

Character Significance refers to the development of the main characters. Let's take Scout in *To Kill a Mockingbird*. Scout is the narrator and thus our window into the world of the racist South in Maycomb, Alabama, in the 1930s. She has a lot to learn about not judging other people until she's walked a mile in their shoes. Over the course of the book, Scout's perspective on Boo Radley and her brother, on her father and Tom Robinson, as well as on the town in which she lives, all change. Together, these changes reflect Scout's developing character. As you read, you need to recognize the moments of change—those moments when Scout learns or reveals something to us about who she is becoming.

Relationship Significance involves the changing dynamics between characters. In *To Kill a Mockingbird*, Scout has several very important relationships. The primary ones are with her brother, Jem, and her father, Atticus. Scout is a careful observer and learns many things from these two male figures, both of whom parent and protect her in different ways. Their relationships, however, are not unchanging. At the beginning of the story, Scout is constantly in Jem's shadow as his little sister, but by the end she has emerged as his equal. Where, when, how, and why does this happen? As you read, you have to look for those moments of relationship development, those significant times when the connections between Jem and Scout change. Another relationship to follow is that of Scout and Boo. Scout is terrified of Boo because of the local legends that circulate among the children of the town. But by the end she has come to understand who Boo really is and she has also become mature enough to treat him with respect. Harper Lee has built that changing dynamic into the book, and your job is to trace its development. Another interesting set of relationships concerns Scout's connection to women. Her mother died when Scout was young, and she grows up without much female influence in her life. Who is supposed to teach her how to "be a woman" in the southern world of that time? What are the positive and negative examples she encounters and how do they shape her own emerging sense of womanhood? Those relationships are fascinating to uncover. Read carefully in order to find them.

Plot Significance refers to how the central events of the story develop. In *To Kill A Mockingbird* Harper Lee presents us with several mysteries that must be untangled: Who is this supposedly terrifying Boo Radley? What really happened between Mayella Ewell and Tom Robinson? Will the jury of Maycomb convict Tom or not? Tracing the turning points in the evolution of these plots is what your reading must focus on. This means that not every episode in the adventures of Scout and Jem has the same importance. The significant moments are those that take what we know and change those preconceptions. What is the precise moment when Scout sees that Boo, whom she thought was haunting her the whole time, is actually a kind of guardian angel? What is the precise moment in the trial when we realize that Tom Robinson is telling the truth, or that Mayella is lying? If you treat what you read like a detective story, then you will always be on the hunt for the "facts of the case." These are the plot points from which you'll be able to reconstruct exactly how the story unfolded.

➢ *SUMMING UP*

Good reading is the essential first step in the writing process. Make sure to have as many thoughts, reactions, likes, and dislikes as you can. Read closely by looking for what's significant with respect to character, relationship, and plot. Read like a detective tracking down the interesting and unusual facts of the case as they twist at key turning points in the plot.

Themes in Literature

Any deep appreciation of a work of literature requires an engagement with the themes the author is exploring. The **theme** is the topic or thrust the writer develops over the course of the book. Even very big books, like Homer's *Odyssey*, have a central theme, which, in the case of this three-thousand-year-old epic, is announced in the very first line: "Sing in me muse and tell me of that man of twists and turns, Odysseus." The twenty-four books (you can think of them as chapters) that follow expand upon what it means to be the wily Odysseus, the man who gets out of tight squeezes by using his wits, thus revealing an important theme that Homer explores—the heroic code: what it means to be a hero in Ancient Greece. Of course there are also other important themes. Penelope is Odysseus' clever and patient wife, who remains faithful to her husband despite having to endure the twenty years of his absence. In Penelope's character and her actions, Homer treats the theme of fidelity. And one further theme: Odysseus' son, Telemachus, grows up without his father and is forced to discover (on his own, but with help from Athena) how to become a man. In Telemachus' story, Homer develops a third theme: self-discovery.

Because literature translates human experience into words, no matter what the work—a novel, a short story, a fairy tale, a play, an epic saga—one may generally say that there are only a certain number of essential themes present in works of fiction:

Love—its difficulties, its grandeur, its unexpected power. So much of fiction explores this theme, but one excellent example is Shakespeare's *A Midsummer Night's Dream*. The lovers Hermia, Lysander, Helena, and Demetrius get all mixed up in a multidimensional love circle, each one chasing after the person he/she thinks he/she loves—only, eventually, to have it all sorted out with the help of the gods, Oberon and Titania (who are going through their own rocky relationship).

Family, and the complex, idiosyncratic relationships in it; what pulls it apart, what brings it together. William Faulkner's *As I Lay Dying* presents some pretty messy family dynamics as Anse Bundren and his children drive the corpse of his wife and their mother, Addie, across Mississippi to be buried. Narrated by each member of the family, the trip reveals the layers of their relationships to Addie and to each other that haunt the past and present. In Lorraine Hansbury's *A Raisin in the Sun*, we see the Younger family struggle with the decision of what to do with the proceeds of a life insurance check from the dead husband and father, Walter. Each has a different idea about how the money will help the family. The play explores the dynamics of power and the struggles among the family members to make a decision and live with its consequences.

Citizenship, including the relationship of the individual to the state; more generally, what is the role of personal freedom against the conventions of society? In Sophocles' *Antigone*, the title character must struggle against her uncle, Creon, who refuses to let her bury her brother because he fought against Thebes, their native city. Where do Antigone's loyalties lie? Do her religious beliefs transcend the laws of the land? To whom does she owe the greatest fidelity: to her dead brother, or to the ruler of her country? How do she and Sophocles resolve this fundamental tension?

Otherness, racism, sexism, have-nots, outsiders. The world has not always been so kind to those it considers not white or male enough, not native, not wealthy. Arthur Miller's *The Crucible* reveals the power of the word "witch" in Puritan Massachusetts in the 1600s. Ralph Ellison's *Invisible Man* presents a black man struggling to be seen as equal in pre-civil rights era America. All of Jane Austen's novels present extraordinary female characters who are learning to navigate their hopes and desires during the formality of England's Regency Period. How do they find appropriate self-expression in this male-dominated world? In the poetry of Edna St. Vincent Millay, she consistently expresses a deep, yearning feminine voice, one that presses against the restrictions of accepted social practice.

War, its horrors, dehumanization, and the destruction it wreaks. Ernest Hemingway's *For Whom The Bell Tolls* paints a vivid picture of the life of partisan guerrillas living behind fascist enemy lines during the Spanish Civil War. The descriptions of the Republicans meting out revenge against the Fascists in the small towns of Spain are detailed, unsparing, and gruesome. (And the Republicans are the good guys!)

Art, the quest for creative self-expression through aesthetic experimentation. Treated broadly, this theme includes the desire to know oneself. Chaim Potok's *My Name is Asher Lev* presents an Orthodox Jewish boy who wants to be a painter, even if it means violating the Jewish traditions his parents have tried to impart to him. How does young Asher come to terms with his desire to paint the crucifixions that are such a central focus of the imagery of the Western aesthetic tradition? In Mark Twain's *Huckleberry Finn*, Huck strives for a way to live by his own inner compass. To find out what he believes, he runs away from violence and repressive education and goes off to have many adventures with Jim, a runaway slave. Huck's growing up and his desire for self-knowledge, much like that of Telemachus in the *Odyssey*, is the journey of an artist.

Money, its vast possibilities, its even vaster pitfalls. F. Scott's Fitzgerald's portrait of the gilded good times in America in *The Great Gatsby* is a prime example of the excesses of money and how wealth is used as a vehicle of social acceptance as well as a way to hide who one truly is.

These are some major theme categories in literature, and within each one you can find an even more specific theme that applies to what you're reading. All books have a specific perspective on the theme, and sometimes even contradictory perspectives. It is that conflict of perspectives that makes the story vibrant and engaging.

Themes in History

Historians treat the idea of theme a little differently. When they look back at a particular era, historians are looking for a shorthand that unites all the happenings of that period of time. For example, in "The Gilded Age" in America those new-fangled business entities called "trusts" and "corporations" led to a business boom, but the benefits all went to the controlling elites —those generally referred to as "robber-barons" who owned the monopolies. The worker, the farmer, and the lowly consumer only got squeezed, paying more for the things they bought. Thus the era was "gilded;" it had the appearance of gold, but it was not so golden underneath that veneer. **Money** as a general theme would certainly be part of any essay on "The Gilded Age," and money would also apply to numerous periods in American History—most notably the 1920s-1930s—when a "roaring" economy bottomed out and led to a decade that historians refer to as the Great Depression, a period of struggle and suffering for many Americans.

The theme of **war** is also well represented in history. Take World War I or II to see the death and destruction that was visited upon Europe and Japan, the many millions of lives lost. **Citizenship** is an issue that hundreds of Supreme Court cases explore: what exactly does the law say and who gets to interpret it? What fundamental rights do Americans have? How do interpretations of the law affect an individual's behavior? For African-Americans, the fight for civil rights is a profound example of the desire for equality and political representation, as it is for American women, who have fought for these rights for themselves for generations.

> ➤ *SUMMING UP*
>
> Every work of literature and every era of history can be said to have a central theme (or a group of themes). General theme categories such as **Love**, **Family**, **Citizenship**, **Otherness**, **War**, **Art**, **Money** can be broken down more specifically to suit whatever you're reading.

Time

Students often ask me how long it should take to read a book. The answer, a not-very-satisfying one, is: I have no clue. Some people read quickly; others read slowly. Some fast readers are actually reading too fast —they're not finding the juicy details, the changes in plot, character, and relationship; they're just trying to get to the end. Reading like that is nearly worthless and probably a waste of time. However, reading too slowly, also has disadvantages: you lose the momentum of the story. Reading too slowly becomes a muddy trudge through the text.

Reading will take as long as it takes you, but the experience of reading will be far more enjoyable if you are **reading actively**—responding to what you read with questions ("He did *what*?"; "She said *what*?"; "How is *that* going to work out?"; "What is this author talking about?"). Do not worry about being able to answer those questions on the spot because they will work themselves out over the course of the story.

> ➤ *QUICK TIP:*
> *BEGINNINGS AND ENDINGS*

There's not always enough time to read every word of a book. Sometimes you have to skim; sometimes you may be forced to the *Cliff's Notes* version. Then there's the internet. No matter. If time is limited, your best friends are **beginnings** and **endings.** Don't get me wrong, what's in the middle is important because it connects the dots between the beginning and the ending. But stories change over time, and merely by taking note of the beginning and ending, you can learn a lot. Let's take Homer's *Iliad*.

The *Iliad* is one long piece of literature. It's epic. It's huge. But the essential story is in the first and last books. In the first, the wrath of the great warrior Achilles overwhelms him, and he stops fighting for the Greeks. In the last, after Achilles has returned to the fighting and killed his arch-enemy, the Trojan hero Hector, Hector's father, Priam, comes to Achilles' tent to beg for the return of his son's body, so he can bury him properly. Surprisingly, Achilles puts aside his wrath and returns the body of his hated enemy. In essence, the entire *Iliad* is about what happens when Achilles gets angry. He cannot control it in the beginning, but he manages to control it in the end. If you read only the beginning and the end, you will lose a wealth of important and enjoyable detail from the middle of the epic, but there's enough in those first and last books to be the subject of an essay.

Whether or not you have time to read the whole book, be sure to react to *specific* things. If you read only the beginning, consider what the story is promising the reader: is it fast-paced or slow? Is it funny or boring? Are the characters good or evil? Smart or stupid? (Or, in either case, neither extreme, but perhaps somewhere in between?) If you can read the ending, too, you can contemplate how the story has changed, how the characters at the beginning were not the same at the end. You may also be led to think about why the author wrote as he did.

➤ *SUMMING UP*

Read actively, looking for detail and asking questions, and always know how a story begins and ends.

2. Taking Notes

A **note** contains important **thoughts** about what you're reading. Taking notes means reading the text actively, with an eye towards distinguishing what is important from what is forgettable—which necessarily means that you must read with a pen or pencil in your hand. It is the pen (and not your brain) that is the instrument of note-taking. Holding a pen in your hand is a crucial part of reading actively.

Of course many students in high school today may read some, if not all, assigned texts digitally. Even so, the necessity of note-taking persists and is, in fact, magnified because the digital experience fades away in an endless scroll or swipe, whereas the hard copy of a book can be flipped through and used as a resource repeatedly.

There is no single best way to take notes by hand, but you want to devise a system that will serve you well when you need to find key passages and meaningful quotations for the essay you'll be writing later. If you find yourself writing down paragraphs of notes, you're probably taking too many. If you're only taking one note per chapter, it's probably too few.

Many students underline the sentences they think important while reading by dragging the pen horizontally below each line of text. This can make the text messy and hard to read, especially if you can't draw perfectly straight lines. Consider making a vertical line to the right or left of the passage you wish to note. It will still draw your eye to the important passage, but it will keep the page neater and more organized. You can also take notes by highlighting with a highlighter. This will keep the text clear and clean and draw your eye directly to the important passages.

I've seen students who don't like to write in their books simply dog-ear the pages they want to revisit. Just fold down the corner flap, and your eye will immediately take note of the important pages when you pick up the book to look for juicy quotes. Otherwise, if you don't like to write in your books, open up a notebook or create a document on your computer and share your thoughts there as you read. If your curriculum is on-line, you probably can use something similar to a "track changes" function in the software to insert your reactions into little text-boxes. Otherwise, you'll want to record your notes on a piece of paper or by typing up a separate word-processing document. If you include page numbers with your reactions to the material, you'll be in good shape when you have to find the significant passages later for the essay.

> ➣ *QUICK TIP:*
> *USING THE MARGINS*

All printed books leave room on all four sides of the text. These "white spaces"— called margins—can be most helpful for note-taking. Margins are excellent for jotting down any thoughts about what you've read.

Suppose the character you thought was the hero does something evil. You could react to that by writing in the margin, "Oh no! Not heroic!" Or perhaps you are tracking the writer's use of language; he keeps repeating the word "flower" in different contexts. In addition to underlining/highlighting the word "flower," you could also write it in the margin and maybe even add a note to remind yourself when the word was last used. For example, "Flower. See p. 42."

The extreme example of using the margins is the Talmud, the ancient Jewish book with the text of the Torah in the center of the page and commentary from rabbis surrounding the text on all four sides. But there is no need to make your marginal notes talmudic! Writing down too many comments in the margins will also make the page messy and harder to decipher what your thoughts were while reading. Do use the margins, but keep those notes short and to-the-point.

For a work of fiction in an English class, I tell my students to take notes on **three important passages per chapter**. Why three? Well, these are (or should be) precisely the ones that tell the story, pushing it onward. One paragraph at the beginning, one in the middle, and one at the end. The three paragraphs should be a kind of mini-chapter that conveys the important developments within the story.

When you're taking notes, remember that you're looking for what's **significant**. You don't need to pay attention to a whole lot of the text, only to what registers a change in **plot**, **character**, and **relationship**.

Above, we looked at *To Kill A Mockingbird*. Now let's look at *The Catcher In The Rye*, by J.D. Salinger, and see what kind of notes we should be taking as we read.

Remember that plot is what happens in a story. In *Catcher*, the main character, Holden Caulfield, is kicked out of boarding school, returns to New York City without telling his parents, puts up at a hotel, heads out on the town, has an adventure with a prostitute, meets up with an old girlfriend to see a play, stays a night with a former teacher who turns out to be a pedophile, tracks down his sister and watches her ride the famous carousel in Central Park. What's significant about any particular episode is how quickly-slowly, how greatly-minimally, the events unfold. You're looking at the action of the story and trying to isolate the important moments. (I skipped over a number of early scenes in which Holden is annoyed at his roommates because I didn't think they were significant plot developments.)

Characters change over time. Holden Caulfield, a jaded adolescent in the midst of some serious growing pains, changes *throughout* the story. What are Holden's reactions to what is happening to him? What is he learning as he lives his life? Look at the prostitute plot point. For Holden, his choice not to sleep with the prostitute, but instead to talk with her and learn about her, says much about the curious, not-quite-sexually active boy he remains underneath his "sophisticated" cynicism. It shows us that Holden is not yet ready to live by his wilder convictions of how an independent, free-thinking adult can behave. Your notes should carefully track these developments in his character. Reading actively will lead you to questions about what Holden learns about himself through his own life experiences. How does what happens affect him?

Finally, tracking the evolution of a relationship through key moments is essential to what is significant in the story. Friendships can be built, and friendships can be broken. Expectations of love and the surprise of betrayal can destroy the lives of the characters. Holden rejects authority, both academic and parental, but his relationships with his siblings are crucial. The guiding light throughout the whole book is his sister, Phoebe, in whom he feels comfortable confiding. When he tells her he is leaving home, she shows up with a suitcase and intends to leave with him. This devotion is touching, but is made more complicated when he refuses—angrily—to take her with him. She cries. Eventually, he takes her to the carousel. As Phoebe rides the carousel, Holden is so happy he almost breaks into tears himself. It's a confusing episode, rich with details about this special bond between these two siblings. Why does Holden refuse to take Phoebe with him? Has he become a pseudo-parent, acting (unbeknownst to her) in his little sister's self-interest? What does the carousel episode reveal about how these siblings wound, care for, or admire each other?

➤ *QUICK TIP:*
IMAGERY

I encourage students to take notes on the **language** and **imagery** of the text. Especially for poetry or for any text that uses elevated language (such as Shakespeare, Homer, Milton, or Joyce), keep track of striking turns of phrase, or of the images the writer presents. What sorts of images keep popping up? Is the writer interested in colors, or is the world of the author covered in black and white? Is one character associated with a particular animal or flower—or something else? Paying attention to, and then remarking on, these specific choices will make your essay interesting and rich with detail.

In *The Catcher In The Rye*, there is a famous passage in which Holden Caulfield reveals his dream: he's standing in a field of rye, trying to prevent children from running over the edge; he's trying to catch them to keep them from falling to their deaths. The catcher in the rye; it's what gives us the very title of the book. Everyone always points out this passage (yawn). But few people discuss a passage from the beginning of the book in which Holden is asked by his roommate, Stradlater, to write a paper for him about an object. Holden chooses his brother's baseball mitt, which he can't use because his brother, Allie, was left-handed. Instead, Holden has saved the glove because of its *emotional* power. The mitt has poems written all over it in green ink because Allie liked to read poetry when he was bored in the outfield. The baseball mitt is used to catch baseballs; but in Holden's dream, he wants to catch children before they fall to their deaths. The real power of the mitt becomes clear when you note that Allie died from leukemia, a death that had a profound effect on Holden. Holden's dream of trying to catch children before they die thus takes on its weighty significance once you know about his dead brother Allie. Tracing the **imagery** of the mitt, and the **language** of "catching," would lead to a nice essay.

For a History assignment, your notes should include all the **key terms** and important historical figures (with dates!). **Time is what tells the story in history**. At the turn of the century, in mid-century, and at the end of the century are the equivalent of beginning, middle, and end. Historians are interested in how things change over time, so make sure your notes keep track of the timing of historical events/figures.

> ➤ *QUICK TIP:*
> *HISTORY IS A GREAT STORY*

Many students report being bogged down by the endless series of dates and details that History textbooks present. This is a real problem, and you can waste a lot of time just trying to memorize names and dates. Good teachers know that what makes History exciting is not a timeline, or a long list of all the battles in a given war, or the entire legislative record of the 43rd Congress.

History is a *story*—a great story—filled with heroes, villains, devastating battles, decisive laws, important social movements. The way to bring it to life is to transform a History lesson into an exciting tale. In your imagination, dramatize the conflicting positions between two presidential candidates. Enter the mind of a military commander about to invade against impossible odds. Relive the experiences of a social activist fighting for justice and equality.

As in all good stories, you should find a beginning, middle, and an end—an excellent structure to help you make sense of all those dates. If you categorize the important dates and events in a beginning-middle-end format, you will find it easier to keep track of the most important dates and to make sense of the entire History lesson.

Take World War II as an example. It is, perhaps, the most significant historical event of the 20th century. There are so many dates, battles, military and political figures to remember. If you don't recreate it in your imagination as an exciting story, you'll easily lose your way. But try *dramatizing* it:

The beginning—The German people were *poor* and *angry* because of the terms of the Treaty of Versailles which ended World War I. They needed to *blame* someone. They needed a leader who reminded them of Germany's former *glory*. Enter Adolf Hitler. Hitler *plotted* his rise to power for many years, staging an unsuccessful coup (the Beer Hall Putsch on November 8, 1923) that landed him in prison. He used the time to write his memoir, *Mein Kampf*, which presented the Germans with a vision of national pride and outlined a *hateful* system of beliefs called Nazism. When he got out of jail, Hitler led the Nazi party to eventual power by combining traditional campaigning with *violent* tactics. Hitler had *thugs* called the "SS" who did his bidding. They *killed* opposition party members and *harassed* Jews, gays, communists, and intellectuals. In 1933, the same year Hitler became Chancellor, the government building, called the Reichstag, *burned* to the ground under suspicious circumstances, allowing Hitler to declare martial law. Hitler's *henchmen* arrested political opponents and began to *oppress* those they deemed inferior. *Infamously*, on November 9, 1938, they *smashed* the windows of Jewish businesses in an episode known as Kristallnacht.

That kind of story is exciting and lively. It weaves together important details in an organized way that gives a sense of the kind of hardship and villainy of Germany in the 1920s and 30s. Now do the same kind of dramatic retelling for the **middle** and **end** of WWII, and you'll have the whole story memorized.

➤ *SUMMING UP*

Take notes that pluck out the significant changes (character, plot, relationship) in what you are reading. Invent your own clean, neat way to draw your attention to the important passages, whether by highlighting, making vertical lines, dog-earing pages, or jotting down reactions in the margins. For English essays, pay attention to the beginning, middle, and end of each chapter as well as the descriptive terms to which the writer returns. When you write an essay for your History class, tell the story by paying close attention to *temporal* relationship, that is, with the way the passage of time affects the course of events. Keep in mind what existed first, how it changed, and how it ended: over the months, years, decades, or centuries. Turn those dates and details into a compelling story.

3. Coming Up With A Question

Who, What, Where, When, How, and Why

Most likely, your teacher will assign you a question to answer. If that's the case, then you have your notes as an initial reference point to see which important **thoughts** (feelings, ideas, hints, reactions) could apply to the teacher's question. Best of all, there are really only so many questions that can be asked.

Who questions are pretty simple. Who shot Kennedy? Who invented the cotton gin? Whom does Darcy love? Flip through your notes or find the text online. Either way, you should be able to find the answer easily.

What questions require precision, but not much exploration. What is the name of Macbeth's wife? What is Achilles' dilemma in the *Iliad*? In *Hamlet*, what do Rosencrantz and Guildenstern agree to do on behalf of the King and Queen? During the US Civil War, what were the North's advantages? What were Woodrow Wilson's Fourteen Points? These questions require answers with specific facts, but no need for much proof or argumentation.

Where questions rely on memorization of somewhat meaningless facts. Where does *Hamlet* take place? Answer: Elsinore. Where did the Battle of Gettysburg in the Civil War take place? Hint: It was not at Antietam.

When questions are even easier. When did Columbus sail the ocean blue? Answer: In 1492.

How and **Why** questions stand somewhat apart from those discussed thus far. Answering these questions will help you dig deeper into the material because they spark your imagination and force you to begin a search for motivation and interpretation.

Take the question "Why does Hamlet act crazily (or at least erratically)?"

There's a complicated answer to that: He suspects that his uncle murdered his father and he wants to find proof. But why *crazy*? Well, by acting as if he were mad, Hamlet is able to turn the world of the court upside down. He's also in a better position to interrogate his friends and relatives in a way that his "normal" self would be unable to. But why does he continue to do so, even when he begins to hurt those he used to love? That question is for you to decide. Perhaps he's not just acting crazy; perhaps he has gone insane. Why Hamlet acts crazy is therefore a fascinating and complex question that makes for an excellent essay. It also leads to a follow-up question: "How does Hamlet's craziness manifest itself?" For the answer to that, you would have to find specific examples of his unsteady behavior.

What if your teacher asked you, "How did the North win the Civil War?" First, winning the war wasn't easy, so there's no simple way to answer this. Yes, the North had economic and infrastructure advantages. There was also more manpower in the North, thus it fielded a larger army. But then why wasn't the war over within a year? Well, there were huge problems with leadership in the North: failed military strategies that cost valuable time. There was also the added difficulty of organizing and executing an invasion, whereas the South could dig in and fortify a defensive position. Eventually, after some mistakes by the South's leading general, Robert E. Lee, the Northern general Ulysses S. Grant was able to exploit some of the North's natural advantages in manpower and resources. How the North won the Civil War is a typical US History question. It requires marshaling many factors of different significance to demonstrate your case. It makes for a great essay.

Compare and Contrast

Some teachers like to ask more open-ended questions. A perfect example is the "Compare and Contrast" question, which is really not a question at all. "Compare and contrast the League of Nations and the United Nations." "Compare and contrast Elizabeth Bennet in *Pride and Prejudice* and Jane Eyre in *Jane Eyre*." Great, but *how* do I compare them and *why* are they different? Yes, you guessed it, compare and contrast questions are just **how** and **why** questions at heart. In order to answer these questions, you need to come up with categories of comparison.

To compare and contrast Elizabeth Bennet and Jane Eyre, think of three ways they behave:

1. How they interact with those they love...
(Are they constant? Are they fickle?)

2. How they go about getting what they want...
(Are they stubborn? Aggressive? Passive?)

3. What they learn about themselves...
(Is it good to be flexible? Is constancy rewarded?)

You could choose other categories, depending on what engaged you about the books, but you must choose three to make your essay convincing.

To compare and contrast The League of Nations and the United Nations, you would need three categories, too:

1. Historical context...
(Why were they created?)

2. What are/were their strengths and weaknesses...
(Inclusiveness vs. Exclusiveness;
Practical vs. Moral Power)

3. Why did one fail and the other succeed...
(Was it the historical period, or did they lack sufficient resources, legal authority, or the commitment by member nations?)

You could have chosen other categories of comparison; any three will do.

> ➤ *QUICK TIP:*
>   *HIDDEN QUESTIONS*

"**To what extent**…" is another teacher favorite that is really just a why/how question. "To what extent is Shakespeare the most important dramatist of the English language?" A broad, sweeping question like this can lead to an unhelpful answer: "To a great extent." But you need to write a whole essay, so you must go further. **Why** is he so important? Because his plays explore a vast terrain of history, psychology, and complex human emotion. And how does he explore this terrain? Shakespeare's characters are not generalized types; they're complicated kings, queens, fathers, mothers, daughters and sons—they are three-dimensional human beings in difficult circumstances. Shakespeare asks questions about honor, loyalty, love, friendship, justice and revenge. Now you've translated "to what extent" into something specific and interesting; in so doing, you have made the question answerable. You must still choose your own specific examples to support your thoughts, but at least you are looking squarely at the question.

Some teachers love "**What is the significance of**…" questions. But this is not a **what** question at all. It's really a **why** question: "Why is such-and-such significant?" Once you know it's really a **why** question, you can begin to assemble your precise and focused thoughts.

If your teacher doesn't assign a specific question, then it's up to you to ask something probing and important about the material. Your best friends are **why** and **how**. But don't misunderstand: you'll need the **who**, **what**, **where**, **when** questions at some point; they will be necessary for you as you provide detail, but they won't jumpstart the imagination like **why** and **how** will.

➤ *SUMMING UP*

There are only so many questions that lead to a good essay, and they all begin with **how** and **why**. Even sneaky questions like **What is the significance of...** and **To what extent...** are really just **how** and **why** in disguise. When asked to compare and contrast, make sure you come up with three categories of comparison.

The Middle of the Writing Process

The **middle** of the writing process also has three essential steps: **brainstorming, outlining**, and **writing a rough draft**.

1. Brainstorming

You've read the novel or poem or textbook (or part of them, at least) and you've taken **notes** (which include important **thoughts**) and you've been asked a question by your teacher, or you've come up with your own. You're ready to write, right?

Wrong. One of the big errors high school students make is starting to write before really knowing what they want to say. The essay that results becomes a bunch of disjointed thoughts, which, though perhaps interesting individually, don't fit together. Before you write, you must do what I call **brainstorming**.

How can you elaborate on your own responses to what you've read? What, in particular, resonates? What seems boring and trite? What did the teacher spend five weeks discussing in class? In contrast, what to you seems underappreciated by your teacher? What about the story specially grips or entertains you? With which characters do you identify? Which do you have no patience for—and why?

It is most important for you to accept that your ideas don't have to fit together right now! These are only your first attempts at answering a deeper, more complicated **why** or **how** question. For the moment, just let the potential answers flow.

I had an English teacher in middle school who taught that the only question worth asking about a book is: **"How does this book relate to the meaning of life?"** I didn't get it back then, but I do now. He meant that literature is intended to touch our lives deeply, to move us by means of a story about people who experience great hardship or great success—and who therefore confront the problems of living and who come up with unexpected answers. If you're stuck and don't know what else to brainstorm about, try answering that question!

In History, it is helpful to try to characterize a particular era in order to get a sense of the larger sweep of time. To rephrase the question from my English teacher: **"How did this period of time change the way people lived?"** Revolutionary America featured growing political engagement and social unrest. Or: the 1850's saw a substantial polarization between North and South, often played out in political battles in new, Western states, such as Kansas, Nebraska, and Missouri. The Progressive Era was a response to the excesses of the Gilded Age: inequality, poor conditions for workers, lack of government regulation. Think about the most important features of the period in History you're studying and about how the dynamic leaders of that period tried to bring about substantive changes in peoples' lives. Or you might focus instead on the efforts of different social groups—women, farmers, factory workers, or African-Americans, for example—to assert their rights and bring about necessary changes.

➤ *QUICK TIP:*

GETTING INTO THE AUTHOR'S HEAD

In English, another wonderful question to spark your imagination is **"Why do you think the author wrote this book?"** Jane Austen could have written anything, but she wrote *Pride and Prejudice.* Samuel Beckett wrote *Waiting for Godot.* William Faulkner wrote *As I Lay Dying.* Why? What about the stories and characters moved the author to write them? What are these wonderful writers saying about their cultures? What do their stories say about life? About love? These may not be easy questions to answer, but brainstorming them should lead you to some big, new thoughts.

When you brainstorm, again, it's best that you don't worry right away about fitting all your ideas together. Just leave room for brainthunder and brainlightning; let your ideas flow out onto the paper or computer screen. One or two of your first thoughts will survive the storm and get you started.

➤ *SUMMING UP*

Don't start writing until you've brainstormed. Ask big questions about the book or the time period. Don't worry at first about having all your thoughts make sense!

2. Outlining

So there they are, your wonderful brainstormed ideas. Now you must choose one or two for development. Or better yet, you must choose the **one that is most important** and several that are less important. The most important one has priority over everything else. It's like the red bullseye in the center of an archery target. Everything you will write is aimed at articulating and supporting that one **bullseye thought**.

Outlining means laying out your ideas in an order that promotes their logical flow, enabling your reader to follow and understand easily. What idea is the most important to you? Put that first and then line up smaller ideas to support it. If an idea doesn't fit with your main idea, put it off to the side. (It might be a great idea, but it might belong to a different essay.) Your essay can only be about one main idea, your bullseye thought. The outlining process will shape your ideas from brainstorming into something clear, strong, and worth reading.

Not to overuse the metaphor, but outlining is a bit like laying out the **skeleton** of your essay—the barest bones of your thoughts from which a human form can be seen, but without the flesh and blood that make it come alive. You don't need to write complete sentences in your outline, but you do have to be clear about what kind of structure you are creating. (The finer points of the five-paragraph essay will be discussed in the following chapter.)

> ➤ *QUICK TIP:*
> *TALKING IT OUT*

In service of outlining, it is often helpful to try to speak your ideas out loud—what I call "talking it out." Even better is if someone is willing to listen to you, but you can also do this alone. Try recording it on your smartphone or computer. Say out loud: "My bullseye thought is X, Y, Z." Play it back. Does it make sense? Ok, then proceed. "In support of that main idea, here is an example, also aimed at the bullseye." Again, listen to what you said. Is it clear? Is it really aimed directly at the center of the bullseye, or will your arrow miss left or right? Talking the thoughts out so that you can hear them will reveal whether your essay is flowing clearly and logically and whether you are getting better at expressing those thoughts concisely. If you—or someone listening to you—can't follow the logic smoothly, or if you notice a "hole" in your reasoning, you have to go back to your reading to find a better piece of evidence, or go back to your brainstorming to find a new idea that flows from your bullseye thought.

The first section of your **outline**—let's call it the "skull" of the skeleton of your essay—is your **introduction**. Your bullseye thought must be clearly expressed in the introduction, along with any other brainstormed thoughts that help set the stage for the reader. Your bullseye thought might be accurate, but it still needs three pieces of supporting evidence that *prove* it right. Briefly mention any evidence in the introduction—in summary form.

The next three parts of your outline are your **body paragraphs**, each of which explores one piece of evidence from your introduction. In your outline, make sure you divide the three pieces of evidence into three different groups, each corresponding to the paragraphs you will write. You should also include page numbers from the passages you intend to cite, so that you can easily use quotations from the text when you begin writing. (Ideally, these quotes will be ones you noted while you read or that the teacher pointed out in class as being important.)

Finally, the last large group of thoughts in your outline is the **conclusion**. Your conclusion should, at this stage, be unknown. You don't necessarily have any conclusions because you haven't yet finished fully expressing your ideas. Why lock yourself into a conclusion now, when it could change later? Instead, restate your **bullseye thought** here. That's what you wanted to focus on in the introduction, and you should still be focused on it. Especially because you're finally about to start writing.

> ➤ QUICK TIP:
> SAMPLE OUTLINE

Let's suppose your History teacher asks, "What is the significance of the Treaty of Versailles in terms of World War II?" First, let's translate the question into **how** and **why**. What your teacher is really asking is: "**Why** is the Treaty of Versailles important to our understanding of World War II? **How** was the treaty a factor in the outbreak of a second world war only twenty-five years after the first world war?"

Your textbook will surely discuss the Treaty of Versailles and its many punitive—and ineffectual—measures to prevent a war like the one it ended. There is a lot of information to work with, and if you don't organize it into a logical flow, your essay will be incoherent. If you've brainstormed to come up with the important details from your textbook, you can now organize those thoughts. Consider the following outline (which uses complete sentences for clarity's sake):

Bullseye thought

The Treaty of Versailles failed to restore lasting peace in Europe.

Introduction

1. In an attempt to restore Europe after one of its most destructive wars, the Treaty of Versailles created as many problems as it solved.

2. The Treaty did end WW I, but it also laid the foundation for future tensions between Germany and the rest of Europe, which would lead to WW II.

3. Three of the most glaring failures were demanding excessive reparations from Germany, establishing an ineffectual global peacekeeping organization, and redrawing the map of Europe—creating smaller, weaker nations that Germany wanted to recapture.

First Paragraph:
Excessive punishment creates anger

1. Victorious allies (America, Britain, France, and Italy) demanded enormous reparations from Germany to punish it for the damage and destruction of Europe.

2. They made Germany admit to guilt in causing the war, which made the German people angry. The Allies also forbade Germany from having an army.

3. The treaty's economic measures were crippling and led to hardship and recession in Germany.

Second Paragraph:
League of Nations has no power

1. American President Woodrow Wilson called for "Fourteen Points" to prevent crises like WW I.

2. One of the "Points" created a global governing body, The League of Nations.

3. The League had no real authority because it had no standing army of its own and its highly democratic mechanisms for resolving conflict led to gridlock and inertia.

Third Paragraph:
Redrawing map leads to German nationalism

1. Versailles Treaty redrew the map of Europe, forcing Germany to give up land.

2. Poland was created from German land; Germany had to give up Alsace-Lorraine to France and recognize Czechoslovakia.

3. German pride was hurt by loss of its territory, laying the foundation for German nationalism.

Conclusion

1. Treaty of Versailles failed to bring Europe into a stable peace.

2. Discontent caused by reparations, War Guilt clause, and anger at loss of land simmered in Germany.

3. No strong international organization was able to prevent Germany from rearming and starting WW II.

➤ *SUMMING UP*

Outlining means choosing one brainstormed bulls-eye thought that takes priority over everything else. As you build the skeleton of your essay, lay out the ideas broadly, in an order that flows smoothly. Introduction, body paragraphs, and a preliminary idea of a conclusion should be clearly marked out on the page.

3. Writing Your Rough Draft

Now you can finally put fingertips to keyboard. If you have completed the reading process, then brainstormed well, and finally sketched a workable outline, you will have completed the skeleton of your essay. Now, as you write, you will focus on adding **flesh and blood** to your skeleton. (More discussion of the rough draft continues in Chapter 2.)

Follow your outline. Whatever must be expressed and explained in the first part of your outline should be expressed first. Whatever comes second should follow. Don't worry too much about each individual sentence: at this point, you are trying to create the entire sweep of the argument, and you don't want to waste time agonizing over prepositions and punctuation (that will necessarily happen later). As you turn your thoughts into sentences, it's best to let them flow. This may mean that some paragraphs spring more fully formed from your head, while others end up seeming deformed and deficient. That's fine. Keep writing.

➤ *QUICK TIP:*
             KEEP MOVING

As you write the **rough draft**, don't spend time worrying about the quality of your writing. Don't agonize about whether you should use the word "show" or the word "portray" or the word "represent." Those are questions for later. Your task now is to begin bringing your thoughts to life. If you don't know where something goes, just write WHERE DOES THIS GO? in your text and keep writing. Or if you know something goes there, but you don't know *what*, just leave a big XXXXXXXX as a placeholder. Or if you can't find the right quote, just write FIND QUOTE and move on. You'll get back to it later.

Writing the rough draft will show you whether the "skeleton" you laid out in your outline is strong enough to support the entire body of your thinking. Perhaps you thought you had ample evidence for a particular paragraph, but it turns out you don't. Well, that's okay. Now you know you'll have to come back and solve that problem later. When you're done with the rough draft, take a rest. You've earned it. You'll want to set aside your writing for a little while.

➤ SUMMING UP

Write the rough draft by sticking to the logic of your outline "skeleton." Write for flow and don't worry too much about specifics; you'll get back to them later. As you add the "flesh" and "blood" paragraphs to the bones, your essay will reveal its strengths and weaknesses.

The End of the Writing Process

The **end** of the writing process has three essential steps: **macro-editing**, **micro-editing**, and **handing it in**.

1. Macro-editing

Ideally, you'll leave behind your rough draft for twenty-four hours before returning to it for some **macro-editing.** Why twenty-four hours? Because you want to approach your draft with fresh eyes and ears, as if you were a completely different person. You want to pretend you're some general reader (or alternatively, that you are your teacher, who will be grading the quality of your work).

I call this the macro-editing phase because you're looking at the large issues in your essay. Are your big ideas clear, or are they too weakly expressed? Is your bullseye thought continuously in sight throughout the essay or do you wander off target? Does your introduction adequately introduce the three pieces of evidence that your body paragraphs explore? Are the body paragraphs full of supporting evidence in the form of quotations or paraphrases of your thoughts?

If you come across any of those big XXXXXXXX sections, now is the time to fill them in with the appropriate thought. Or perhaps what you thought was missing doesn't actually apply anymore; if so, simply erase it. For the FIND QUOTE sections, this is the time to find those significant passages you noted earlier. If your big ideas aren't clear, or if they are not making sense, this is the right time to rewrite your sentences to restore the logical flow of thought. Maybe you need to cut out one piece of evidence that isn't working and go back to your brainstorm page to find a better thought. Do that now.

Finally, you'll come to your conclusion, which is still a bit of a question mark. You wrote your **bullseye thought**, but you didn't conclude anything from writing the rough draft because you were in the middle of the process and didn't know what to conclude. Now is the time to take a stab at it. Where have your thoughts led you? What is this essay really about? What's the one thing you want a reader to learn?

➤ *SUMMING UP*

After setting aside your rough draft for twenty-four hours, approach it with fresh eyes for macro-editing. Make sure the big ideas and your chosen examples all support your bullseye thought. Take a stab at the conclusion.

2. Micro-editing

Call this phase what you will: polishing, scrubbing, proofreading. It's all aimed at the same thing: creating a **smooth flow of the words** that best convey your thoughts. You want one thought to lead to the next, logically and effortlessly. You want to make your ideas appealing and irrefutable, without typos, grammatical errors, or clunky language that would slow down the reader's appreciation of your thoughts. Most important, you want to express yourself in as few words as possible. This writing principle is called **economy**. Just like money, you have to be careful how you spend your words. Remember how it feels to read a long textbook? Well, your teacher feels the same way about essays that are longer than they need to be.

I tell my students to micro-edit by **reading slowly and out loud** to themselves. Listening to yourself as you read is essential. If you find yourself stumbling over an unnecessarily repeated word, or if the thought makes no sense or points the reader in the wrong direction, you will *hear* it as you read your text aloud. You read your text out loud to involve as many senses as possible in the editing process: your eyes see the shape of the words on the page; your lips pronounce the words and express the rhythm of the thoughts; your ears listen to the flow of sentences. If your eyes lose their place on the page, or your lips stumble over the words while reading, or your ears can't process what they've heard, then the writing is not smooth, and you must edit the sentence.

Now, as you read through your essay, pay close to attention to the **prose style**, which is a fancy term for the way you choose to express yourself in words. Maybe the idea is clear, but the sentence is just too long: it takes too much effort to read and slows the reader down. Break the sentence into two. Or perhaps your sentences are too short: they don't build momentum. Try combining two short sentences into one.

When I work with students on their writing, I often find myself talking about the three meals of the day: breakfast, lunch, and dinner. I am not trying to tell them that I am hungry. Rather, I am pointing out that we don't eat all of our meals in one sitting. Why? Because it would be painful to try to digest that much food at one time. Similarly, when writing, you don't want to overwhelm your reader by asking him to digest too much at one time. So when I tell my students **Breakfast, Lunch, and Dinner**, it is a reminder to them that they should space out their thoughts over the course of a couple of sentences, rather than trying to force all their ideas into one mouthful.

For example, consider the following sentence about John Milton's *Paradise Lost*: "Although Satan is clearly evil and tempts Adam and Eve to disobey God's commandments, Adam and Eve are not completely innocent, either, and Satan is still portrayed in a somewhat positive light because he legitimately feels that God diminished his stature in favor of Jesus." Whoa. What a mouthful! Lots of good ideas, but no **progression of thought**. The sentence above could be broken up into three separate sentences—the smaller morsels are easier to digest.

➤ *QUICK TIP:*
KEYWORDS

I tell my students to use **keywords** to help them smoothly express the development of their thoughts. There are several kinds of keywords:

Ordinal Keywords, such as "First...," "Second...," and "Third..." provide an easy path to follow. Or try "First...," "Next...," and "Last..." These are excellent when you are laying out pieces of evidence.

Temporal Keywords are helpful, too: "*Before* the first dance..." or "*During* the play..." or "*While* they are talking..." or "*When* he shouts loudly..." These indications of time help the reader understand context and are great for setting up quoted text.

Causal Keywords, such as "In order to..." and "As a result..." and "So that..." or "Because of..." are also particularly useful because they connect cause and effect and therefore help one idea flow into the next.

Comparative Keywords set up helpful distinctions: "His sister, *however*..." and "*Instead of* fighting..." and "*Although* she likes him..." and "*In contrast to* Hamlet..." These keywords make your argument easier to follow and help the reader make sense of specific perspectives.

Reinforcing Keywords drive home your point: "In fact...," "Moreover...," "For...," "Indeed...," "Similarly...," "In addition..." Keywords like these serve as hammers, applying force to your thoughts.

Proofreading is not much fun, but it is *essential*. You don't want to waste your teacher's time—or test her patience—correcting your commas. You want her paying attention to the excellence of your ideas. Teachers who spend too much time fixing punctuation get the sense (and perhaps rightly so) that the student completed his work carelessly. Poor punctuation is a fast track to a lower grade, so put the commas in yourself. If there's a standard form for citation, make sure you're using it.

Last of all, you must now put the finishing touches on the conclusion. By now you've read through your essay twice, once for macro-editing and once for micro-editing. You should have a pretty good idea of what your conclusions are. (More conclusion tips are discussed in the next chapter.)

> ➢ **SUMMING UP**
>
> Micro-edit by reading slowly and out loud so that the sentences flow together. If you stumble while reading, chances are it's because there's a problem with the writing. Go back to that spot and find a better way to say it. If your sentences are too long, shorten them to vary the rhythm of the writing. Fix any typos, grammatical errors, or comma problems. Change words that you repeat unnecessarily. Use keywords to shape your thoughts and to make them more persuasive. Finish your conclusion.

3. Print it out and hand it in

The easiest part. You have completed the writing process. Congratulations!

Clarity and Originality

For any High School essay, there are two essential goals to keep in mind: be clear and be original. If you can do both, your teacher will hold you in the highest regard because you haven't wasted his time and you've made him look like he's actually taught you something. But of the two, **Clarity** is far more important than **Originality**.

Clarity means saying exactly what you think in as few words as possible; choosing specific textual evidence to support your argument; and providing a progression of thoughts that anyone—even a ten-year-old—can follow.

Originality is trickier. It means having a personal engagement with your material; having a unique perspective on a character or a story; and striving for an idea that no one else has ever had—even if that idea is far-fetched or simply wrong. (Be careful of original ideas that are also *completely* wrong.)

I tell my students to **be clear in the introduction and original in the conclusion**. Clarity in the introduction puts the reader on the right path, but once there, you need a new thought about why going there was important. If you have expressed yourself clearly, you'll get a B+ or an A-. If your essay is clear *and* original, you'll get an A.

Bad Writing

Bad writing is painful to read and it usually takes several forms. It can be grammatically incorrect; it can be punctuated poorly and contain many misspelled words; it can list a whole bunch of ideas and make no connections between them; it can be vague and repetitive; it can fail to include specific examples that support your claims.

One obvious example of bad writing in High School essays is **overwriting**. The student doesn't know what he wants to say, so he starts fidgeting with cool functions in his writing software, like the thesaurus button. The next thing he knows, he's dressing up bad ideas with fancy words. Instead of being clear, he's being *florid**. Instead of being original, he's being *idiosyncratic**, and the reader cannot grasp the main idea of the essay. **Don't use fancy words.** Say exactly what you mean as if you were talking to a ten-year-old. A ten-year-old wants candy, not a *confection**. Besides, using fancy words makes your teacher work too hard and will prevent him or her from enjoying your essay. You won't achieve *ratiocination**; you'll fail.

* *florid, adj.* — elaborately or excessively intricate or complicated.
* *idiosyncratic, adj.* — of or relating to idiosyncrasy; peculiar or individual.
* *confection, noun* — a dish or delicacy made with sweet ingredients.
* *ratiocination, noun* — a reasoned train of thought.

Another pernicious (sorry... harmful) habit to avoid is **repetition**. Repeating the same idea over and over will not make it stronger. In fact, it makes the idea absurd and uninteresting. Ultimately, repetition doesn't help the reader get anywhere. Worse, it feels like nagging. Bad essays get stuck on one idea and then repeat it every other sentence. Good ideas don't need to be repeated; they need to be *supported*—with evidence! Go back to your outline and see how you can arrange the flow of thoughts so they lead from the first, to the next, to the last—without repeating the same ideas.

Bad writing also suffers from being **vague**. Vague writing is somewhat like overwriting except without the fancy words. Vague writers settle for conventional, surface-level, or superficial insights. Their arguments remain broad—so broad as to be irrefutable, but also so obvious as to be unhelpful. Yes, Shakespeare is a fantastic writer of both comedies and tragedies. Everyone knows that. What do you want to say about that? *How* or *why* is his writing fantastic? Vague writing stays too general and bland, and it reveals a lack of thought. If you find you're being vague, go back and brainstorm some more! Wherever the good ideas are, you haven't found them yet. You must dig deeper and be more specific.

Some students make up for their lack of clear and original thoughts by making outrageous claims. This is called **hyperbole**, or overexaggeration. "William Shakespeare is the greatest writer of all time." "Genghis Khan was the most brilliant military strategist who ever lived." "The United Nations is the most important peace-keeping force in the world." These claims might be true, but this kind of extravagant argumentation has no place in your essay. Claims such as these cover so much ground and lack so much focus that your essay is destined to devolve into bluster without evidence. Instead, go back to your old friends, How and Why. Why is Shakespeare the greatest writer of all time? How did Genghis Khan manage to conquer so much territory? How does the United Nations try to maintain peace in the world? Wild and hyperbolic claims are the hallmarks of an arrogant writer. Of course, you do want to be bold about your thoughts. But be *specific* as well as bold. Don't promise more than you can possibly deliver.

Finally, bad writing often relies on **colloquialism**; it lacks the necessary formal sophistication of an essay. There's a difference between a conversation and writing. In a conversation, you can use intonation and body language and phrases like "you know what I mean" to convey your thoughts. You can see in real time whether your fellow conversationalist is following you (by nodding his head) or is daydreaming (by rolling his eyes to the back of his skull). With an essay, you can't get that instant feedback. You get one chance to make your point, so you must be aware of how you're expressing yourself. Colloquial expressions, such as "good to go," or "barking up the wrong tree," or "not the man he used to be" don't convey information clearly or specifically. If your writing suffers from colloquialisms, you can catch it during the micro-editing phase, when you read your text out loud and listen to the flow of the words. Remove these bland generalizations before they become that dreaded curse of writing, the **cliché**.

I once had an excellent teacher who always told us, jokingly: "Avoid clichés like the plague." It's funny because "to avoid something like the plague" is a cliché that is meant to express just how bad that "something" is. It's a cliché that warns about how bad it is to use clichés. They're bad in formal writing because they lower the specificity of the text to the level of informal speech. An essay is not an example of informal speech! You're not "shooting the breeze" with the reader; you're engaging her in a clear flow of thought. (Yes, thoughts. Remember them?)

➤ SUMMING UP

An excellent essay will be **clear** (especially in the Introduction) and **original** (especially in the Conclusion). Avoid the traps of bad writing: **overwriting**, unnecessary **repetition**, **vagueness**, **hyperbole**, and **colloquialism**. If you're using fancy words, you're probably not focused on your good ideas. If you're just repeating the same thought over and over, you're nagging the reader to death. If you're using clichés, you're not being specific.

CHAPTER 2

The Five-Paragraph Essay

Now you have a clearer understanding of the writing process: how it begins with reading, brainstorming, and outlining, and how it ends with writing a rough draft, followed by macro-, then micro-editing. But what may not be clear yet is exactly *how* your excellent, noted, brainstormed thoughts fit into an essay structure that helps prove your argument. **Structure can feel limiting, but it is your best friend.** The inherent limits of the essay form require you to compress and focus your thoughts into a structure that will be recognizable to your teacher. That form is called **The Five-Paragraph Essay.**

Here is a closer look at the writing of a sample essay draft. How do you lay out the argument from the outline? How do you know if your evidence is good enough? How do you fit your ideas into an **introduction**, **body paragraphs**, and a **conclusion**?

The Five-Paragraph Essay

Introduction, three body paragraphs, conclusion. It's a winning formula and will be the basic model for all suggested essay structures that follow. Because high school essays are generally less than five pages, **The Five-Paragraph Essay** may be the only kind of essay you'll ever need to write (in high school, at least).

Remember when I said that your outline has to line up all your evidence and quotations behind one main thought, the **bullseye thought**? Similarly, think of the Five-Paragraph Essay as an **archery contest**. First, you must aim for the **bullseye**; then you get **three arrows** to hit it; finally, you **tally your score**.

Taking Aim: The Introduction and The Thesis

If you've ever used a bow and arrow, you know that taking aim requires these steps: holding the bow, you notch one arrow; then you raise your bow arm up to shoulder height and draw back the string with your other hand. Finally, you hold the bowstring taut as you look down the range at the multi-colored target, aiming at the red bullseye in the center.

Your **introduction** must do the same thing: set the reader's sights at the bullseye. What are your arrows? They're your three examples (three pieces of evidence) all aimed at hitting the center of the target. You'll want these arrows to have sharp points and to fly straight through the air. What's the bowstring that pulls that arrow taut? The bowstring is your thesis.

Thesis is a fancy word for "argument." And argument is just a fancy word for "perspective"—and that's just a fancy way of saying "your point." **What's your point in writing?** What's the one, single takeaway idea you want the reader to know immediately? (Remember that in our outline, this was called the **bullseye thought**.) The thesis must be clear (just as the bowstring must be taut), or else the arrow won't fly through the air, but flop somewhere on the ground. Everything that follows in the essay will be in support of your clear thesis. (As a bonus, your thesis can also be original, but first it must be clear.) If you don't point the arrow in the right direction now, at the very beginning, it will never reach its target.

Follow these simple rules for an introduction:

1. The first sentence includes the author's name and the title of the work you're writing about and makes a claim (your bullseye thought! your clear point!) about the book.

2. The next three sentences summarize three pieces of evidence (three arrows) supporting that claim.

3. The final sentences restate the opening claim as a thesis, pulling the bowstring taut and ready to launch the reader into the essay.

Maybe you'll need more than one sentence for each piece of evidence. Fine. Maybe you can combine all three pieces of evidence into one sentence. Fine. But you must clearly lay out these three pieces of evidence and point the reader at the target.

> ➢ *QUICK SAMPLE ESSAY:*
> *INTRODUCTION WITH THESIS*

(1.) In William Shakespeare's *Hamlet*, the Danish prince, Hamlet, frequently acts in a dangerous and unsteady manner. **(2.)** He verbally abuses his one-time girlfriend, Ophelia, later causing her to go crazy and commit suicide. While he confronts his mother in her bedroom, Hamlet mistakenly, but brutally, murders Ophelia's father, Polonius. After having his best friends, Rosencrantz and Guildenstern, killed, he later challenges Ophelia's brother, Laertes, to a duel and kills him, too. **(3.)** Hamlet's madness grows steadily, killing many in its path, until it is unclear whether he is just acting crazily or has legitimately gone crazy. Although his quest is noble (he wants to find out who killed his father), Hamlet's physically and emotionally destructive behavior demonstrates the dangers to oneself and to one's community of a fractured identity.

Now, I will not win a Nobel or a Pulitzer Prize for this introduction/thesis. But I will have achieved the first and most important goal of high school essay-writing: clarity. I have a clear perspective, and my three specific examples support my claim. I have pointed my arrows squarely at the bullseye thought. Best of all, I've used simple language and avoided any kind of overblown, fancy wording. I've also avoided repetition and steered clear of generality, colloquialism, vagueness, and cliché. Good for me.

Firing the Arrows: Three Body Paragraphs

One nice thing about archery contests is you get three chances to hit the bullseye. Maybe the first arrow misses low. Well, fine, you can aim a little higher next time. Maybe you aim too far right; then aim more left. With three arrows, you can at least surround that bullseye.

The body paragraphs lay out in detail the **excellent examples** that support your claim. They provide evidence—that which proves your thesis to be true. Presumably, you based your thesis on specific reactions to what you read (your thoughts!), so now you must find the author's specific words to use as proof.

Because many students don't read actively or take clear notes that keep track of their reactions, it can be difficult to find quotations from the text to use as evidence in the body paragraphs. Such a student ends up repeating the arguments from the introduction over and over and over without ever providing the necessary examples. The result is an essay that is repetitive without being informative. A claim has been made, but in the end, nothing has actually been proven—there is no supporting evidence.

Avoid repetition by quoting the text as much as possible. If it's a quotation, it can't be wrong! If it's written in the book (and related to the topic of your essay), then it is irrefutable and will support your argument. Best of all, when you use quotes from the book, you don't have to write as much. Let the author do the work for you.

Follow these simple rules for a body paragraph:

1. Begin with a topic sentence that introduces one piece of evidence (one arrow) and which sets the stage for the discussion in the paragraph.

2. Supply a little context for your quote (i.e. where the quote appears in the book and what has happened before the quote that led up to this moment).

3. Write the quote, in quotation marks, with citation (i.e. Act III.34-46 or page 134).

4. Set down simple statements that explain why your quote proves your argument (try "pulling" individual words or phrases from the big quotation to weave into your statements).

> ➢ *QUICK SAMPLE ESSAY:*
>
> *BODY PARAGRAPH WITH QUOTE*

(1.) One of the first instances of Hamlet's erratic behavior occurs in Act III, when he confronts Ophelia in the palace and treats her rudely. **(2.)** Earlier in the play, Hamlet's mother, Gertrude, and uncle, Claudius, devise a plan to spy on Hamlet because they are concerned about him. The plan has several parts. First, Claudius and Polonius are to hide in the palace hallway, then Ophelia is to let herself be discovered by Hamlet. Finally, Claudius and Polonius are to observe the interactions in order to understand the cause of Hamlet's disturbance. In the hallway, when he confronts Ophelia, Hamlet reveals he is not behaving rationally because he denies having sent love letters to Ophelia and questions her honesty. **(3.)** Indeed, the interaction builds until Hamlet snaps at Ophelia: "Get thee to a nunnery. Why wouldst thou be a / breeder of sinners? I am myself indifferent honest; / but yet I could accuse me of such things that it / were better my mother had not borne me..." (Act III, Scene 1, 121-124). **(4.)** Hamlet has never spoken this way to Ophelia before. Moreover, the reproach is of a very different nature from the love letters he used to send. He first says that he is "indifferent honest," then he accuses himself of "such things" so damning that it would have been better if he had never been born. Finally, Hamlet's insult that Ophelia wishes to be a "breeder of sinners" is particularly harsh. She has done nothing to deserve it. Indeed, Hamlet's motivation for treating Ophelia so unjustifiably is puzzling. If not mad, he is being deliberately cruel.

Again, no literary prizes here, just a clear example from the play that completely supports my thesis. I avoided repetition, I steered clear of colloquialism, I used a quote so I didn't have to write as much, I "pulled" individual words or phrases from the quote as I analyzed it, and I explained why my quote supported my thesis. Everything in the paragraph is aimed right at my bullseye: Hamlet's strange behavior.

If this is not yet clear enough, take a look at the same text, with all my **keywords** now in bold:

(1.) One of the **first** instances of Hamlet's erratic behavior occurs in Act III, **when** he confronts Ophelia in the palace and treats her rudely. **(2.) Earlier** in the play, Hamlet's mother, Gertrude, and uncle, Claudius, devise a plan to spy on Hamlet **because** they are concerned about him. The plan has several parts. **First**, Claudius and Polonius are to hide in the palace hallway, **then** Ophelia is to let herself be discovered by Hamlet. **Finally**, Claudius and Polonius are to observe the interaction in order to understand the cause of Hamlet's disturbance. In the hallway, **when** he confronts Ophelia, Hamlet reveals he is not behaving rationally **because** he denies having sent love letters to Ophelia and questions her honesty. **(3.) Indeed**, the interaction builds until Hamlet snaps at Ophelia: "Get thee to a nunnery. Why wouldst thou be a / breeder of sinners? I am myself indifferent honest; / but yet I could accuse me of such things that it / were better my mother had not borne me..." (Act III, Scene 1, 121-124). **(4.)** Hamlet has never spoken this way to Ophelia before. **Moreover**, the reproach is of a very different nature from the love letters he used to send. He **first** says that he is "indifferent honest," **then** he accuses himself of "such things" so damning that it would have been better if he had never been born. **Finally**, Hamlet's insult that Ophelia wishes to be a "breeder of sinners" is particularly harsh. She has done nothing to deserve it. **Indeed**, Hamlet's motivation for treating Ophelia so unjustifiably is puzzling. If not mad, he is being deliberately cruel.

The keywords have helped shaped all my thoughts and connected them so that the writing flows. I've notched my first arrow, aimed, and fired. When I do this two more times, with my second and third examples of Hamlet's madness, I will have completed all three body paragraphs.

Tallying the Score: The Conclusion

So you've written the intro and three body paragraphs and successfully argued your thesis. Moreover, your three examples prove you're right, using irrefutable quotations. **So what?** That's the question your **conclusion** should try to answer: So you're right. Why should the reader care? If all your arrows have been aimed at the bullseye, it's time to tally the score and see what it all adds up to.

Most students use the concluding paragraph merely to repeat the thesis, which makes the essay bland and repetitive. Worse, it feels as if you haven't taken the reader anywhere. You do need to restate your argument (your **bullseye thought**), but you also must go one step further. **Explain why your argument matters**.

Because most books in a high school English curriculum have been read for decades, if not centuries, it's highly unlikely that your essay has added to humanity any significant understanding of the book in question—but that doesn't matter. What's important here is not to hold on to your argument too tightly—as if you've proved something heretofore unknown. Your thesis isn't the only correct one. Let go of being right and focus instead on *why* your idea is important to the reader. **Why is your thesis essential to understanding this literary masterpiece?**

Scholars have been studying Shakespeare's *Hamlet* for centuries, and more ink has been spilled on the subject of Hamlet's madness than Hamlet spills blood in the play. I'm not a genius for claiming that Hamlet goes mad, but I can put some originality into why I think his madness is essential to understanding the world that Shakespeare created.

➤ *QUICK SAMPLE ESSAY:*

CONCLUSION

Hamlet's madness can be clearly traced over the course of the play. He finally succeeds in his revenge by killing Claudius, but his wild actions also lead to the deaths of others, including his mother and, ultimately, to his own death. Madness, it seems, does not end well for the Danish prince, and the gruesome end of the play is in many ways a warning against the dangers of a fractured identity. Shakespeare, however, has something more important in mind. In Act II of the play, Polonius mutters an important aside during a conversation with Hamlet: "Though this be madness, yet there is / method in 't" (Act II, Scene 2, 195-196). Madness with method, then, is what Shakespeare highlights as Hamlet's crucial strategy in his quest for revenge. Hamlet keeps Polonius, Claudius, and Gertrude guessing, finding great power in feigning a madness that best suits his ends as he seeks to uncover the truth surrounding his father's murder. What Shakespeare suggests, therefore, is that madness can be an important tool. In *Hamlet*, madness and sanity exist fluidly within one person. They are not black and white, but rather part of a dangerous continuum—one that brings the truth to light, but leaves tragedy in its wake.

A conclusion like that—while still not winning any prizes—will delight a teacher with a new spin on an old idea.

I began this sample essay simply, and with a straightforward thesis: Hamlet acts in a dangerous and unsteady manner. I've concluded with a discussion of the purpose of madness in the Shakespearean hero's quest for truth. Not bad for a high school English class! I only used one fancy word: "continuum," which is a noun that means "a continuous sequence in which adjacent elements are not perceptibly different from each other, although the extremes are quite distinct." As I tally my score in the conclusion, I can safely say that my arrows hit the bullseye.

➤ SUMMING UP

The Five-Paragraph Essay provides an easy-to-use structure: Introduction, Three Body Paragraphs, Conclusion. In the introduction, take aim at your bullseye thought with a clear thesis. In the three body paragraphs, fire your arrows of evidence—all aimed at the bullseye and with help from quotations. In the conclusion, be original! Don't just repeat your thesis; explain why your argument matters to someone who is trying to understand and appreciate the book.

CHAPTER 3

Structure

Just as there are only so many questions that can lead to an essay, there are only so many types of essays that can be written. Your essay need not be a whole new creation. Provable arguments have certain essential structures, and there is limited variation within those structures.

In my years of helping students, I've discovered there are only three types of five-paragraph essays that a high schooler really needs to learn: **The Goldilocks Essay**, **The Change Over Time Essay**, and **The Compare And Contrast Essay**. Similarly, there are three bad essay structures to avoid at all costs: **The Frankenstein Essay**, **The Lemming Essay**, and **The Emperor's New Clothes Essay.** Let's start with the good first.

Good Essay Structures

These good structures make it easy to lay out the skeleton of an argument. You add the flesh and blood depending on what your essay is about, but the bones are already in a good, solid form. With your arrows aimed at the bullseye, it's hard to miss when you follow these structures.

The Goldilocks Essay

Everyone knows the fairy tale "Goldilocks and the Three Bears." To summarize: Walking in the woods, Goldilocks stumbles upon a house. She enters to find everything in threes: three bowls of porridge, three chairs, three beds. She tries them out one by one, determining one to be too *this* (hot, big), one to be too *that* (cold, small) and one to be *just right*. After eating the just-right-temperature bowl of porridge, she falls asleep in the just-right-sized bed. Little does she know the house belongs to a family of bears, who return home and chase her away. (In some versions of the story, poor Goldie gets eaten, and a costly lesson about breaking and entering is learned the hard way, but that's not important to us.)

Too big, too small, just right. What a great essay structure that fits exactly into our Five-Paragraph Essay format. Your first body paragraph explains why one argument doesn't quite fit. It's too big. The second body paragraph explains why another argument doesn't quite fit. It's too small. The third body paragraph explains why your argument is just right. Add your introduction (clear roadmap) and conclusion (original response) and you're all set.

In a class on 19th century literature, for example, you might get this question: "In *Pride and Prejudice*, by Jane Austen, why does Elizabeth Bennet choose Mr. Darcy?"

A **why** question like this will be best answered in three body paragraphs that explore Elizabeth's potential love matches.

1. Why does Elizabeth reject Mr. Collins' proposal (he's too stodgy)?

2. Why does Elizabeth at first reject Mr. Darcy's proposal (he's too haughty)?

3. Why does Elizabeth finally accept Darcy (what makes him just right?)?

Your three arrows point squarely at the bullseye: Elizabeth's quest for the appropriate love match. One potential match, to Mr. Collins, clearly aims too low. Another potential match, to Mr. Darcy, first aims too high. The third potential match, again to Darcy, is a direct bullseye. Just right.

The **clarity** of this essay relies on a good thesis: Elizabeth is unlucky in love until she learns to overcome her prejudices and see Darcy as he really is. The originality of this essay will be in how you describe Elizabeth's changing character, based on your thoughts and reactions while reading. What do *you* hate about her in the beginning (supported by some excellent quotations from the beginning of the novel)? What do *you* love about her in the end (supported by some excellent quotations from the end of the novel)? What do *you* think she learns?

Your conclusion should elevate your essay by proposing an answer to the following question: **Why does all of this matter to Jane Austen?** What is her commentary on the social forces and the personal failings that can get in the way of a worthwhile love relationship?

What about a common question from 19th century US History: "To what extent was Gettysburg the turning point of the Civil War?" This "**to what extent**" question is really just a **why** question, and again, we see the Goldilocks trilogy: too big, too small, just right. A good essay here requires three body paragraphs that explore three battles that were potential turning points.

1. Why was Antietam not the turning point (it was bloody, but too early in the war)?

2. Why was Vicksburg not the turning point (it was out West, didn't involve Lee)?

3. Why was Gettysburg just right (Lee was defeated strategically, plus the emotional weight of Gettysburg Address)?

The three arrows point squarely at the bullseye: important battles in the Civil War. One battle was too early, before the scope of the war had truly unfolded. One battle was out West, far from the heart of Robert E. Lee's forces. Only Gettysburg fits just right: victory and defeat in that battle was the true turning point in the war.

The clarity in this essay will emerge from setting up the comparisons in your introduction: "Some battles, like Antietam, were bloody and showed that the South could stand up to the Northern invaders despite fewer resources of personnel and munitions. Other battles, like Vicksburg, were huge tactical successes for the North, but since they took place out West, they did not deal any direct blow to the main Confederate forces. While the outcomes of many battles held clear advantages for either the North or the South, only Gettysburg offered definitive proof that the North could win, both on the battlefield and in Lincoln's soaring, influential rhetoric of the Gettysburg Address after the battle was over."

Your conclusion can elevate this essay by discussing why Gettysburg mattered to someone like Abraham Lincoln. What did the military victory enable him to do politically? It gave him the strength to pronounce the Emancipation Proclamation, because it showed that the North had the military authority it needed to impose laws on the South. Further, Lincoln immortalized Gettysburg in his famous address and rallied the North emotionally for the struggles yet to come. Without a Northern victory at Gettysburg, none of this would have been possible.

The Goldilocks Essay puts the argument clearly in front of the reader. Too big, too small, just right. Try it out and apply it to essay questions you might be asked.

The Compare And Contrast Essay

As I said earlier, the "compare and contrast" prompt offers a bland, general, and, frankly, redundant question that implicitly requires you to translate it into a **how** and **why** essay. To write this essay, you must choose **three categories of comparison**. These will narrow the vast scope of the question to three provable pieces—and they will also be the basis for the three body paragraphs of your five-paragraph essay.

For example, in a challenging high school English class, you might get this question: "Compare and Contrast Odysseus and Achilles in Homer's *Odyssey* and *Iliad*." That is a huge question, which, if you don't break it down into categories, will lead to your wasting years of your life writing a grad school dissertation.

Instead, choose three categories to focus on:

1. How they treat women (Odysseus and Calypso vs. Achilles and Briseis).

2. How they defeat their enemies (Odysseus' cunning vs. Achilles' skill in battle).

3. How they act as leaders (Odysseus quest to reach home vs. Achilles' refusal to fight).

The three arrows you notch are all aimed at the bullseye: what kind of heroes are Achilles and Odysseus? The first and second categories will lead to a good contrast: Odysseus and Achilles treat their concubines differently; Odysseus is the man of many wiles, whereas Achilles is a swift and brutal warrior on the battlefield. The third category will lead to a good comparison: through sometimes selfish or faulty leadership, both Odysseus and Achilles bring about the deaths of many of their fellow Greeks.

But your conclusion must confront a bigger question: why do these two heroes matter to Homer? What is he saying about the role of the hero in the ancient world? This is where your **originality** can shine through: each of your three arrows has hit the bullseye in comparing/contrasting these two preeminent heroes, but now it's up to you to tally the score in the conclusion. Consider, perhaps, that Homer's perspective on what is right and wrong might be a little different from the way our present mainstream culture thinks. How did an Ancient Greek think about these two heroes? Which would he have aspired to become? Which would he have condemned? (Hint: to dig a little deeper, it might be worth rereading a famous conversation between the two heroes in Book XI of the *Odyssey*.)

In History classes, you'll often come across compare and contrast questions because they're great tools for historians to measure the factors that lead to periods of war and peace, dynamic civilizations on the rise and decadent civilizations on the brink of collapse, or excellent leaders and brutal autocrats.

For example: "Compare and contrast what arguably were three of the most powerful leaders of the mid-twentieth century: Adolf Hitler, Josef Stalin, and Mao Zedong."

This is a huge, and fascinating, question. Many books have been written about these famous leaders, so you must find ways to focus your essay. Start by choosing your categories. For Hitler, Stalin, and Mao —all three were leaders of totalitarian regimes—your categories are easy to identify:

1. Economic policies (How did they try to drive economic production? How did they balance agriculture and industry?)

2. Military policies (How did they change their militaries? Were they successful?)

3. Social policies (What restrictions did they put on their people? What new laws? Who was punished and who was persecuted?)

Your success in this compare/contrast essay will rely on two aspects: first, setting up your introduction with complete **clarity**; second, having the facts from your notes/outlines to keep each body paragraph focused on the category in question. Treat one category at a time; don't let them bleed together.

In your conclusion, some **originality** is much to be desired, and you must take into account why your analysis matters. Remember that a shift in perspective is always refreshing. Thus far, your essay has demonstrated your command of the facts, but of course, these three leaders were not just data; they were real people, guided by fiercely held ideologies (for Hitler, Nazism, and for Mao and Stalin, Communism). A discussion about the danger of extreme political viewpoints would be welcome in the conclusion. How did these leaders destroy the opposition and thereby inflict war, poverty, and devastation both on their own people and on the world?

Here's another example, this time from American History: "Compare and contrast the presidencies of John Adams and Thomas Jefferson." To answer this essay on the second and third presidents of the United States, you must, again, choose three categories to compare and contrast. Try these three:

1. Foreign Policy (How did they engage the United States with the international community? Were they successful?)

2. Economic Policy (What laws, taxes, tariffs were passed that promoted/restricted trade and production?)

3. Military Policy (What did they do to strengthen American influence out West, in South America, or abroad? How did they deal with setbacks?)

The beauty of choosing clear categories like these is that you don't need to overwrite to prove your point. Your introduction can be straightforward: you can simply lay out the three categories you're going to explore. Here again, the contrasts leap out without too much research. For foreign policy, Adams was embroiled in an international scandal, called The XYZ Affair, that almost led to war with France; Jefferson, on the other hand, successfully negotiated the Louisiana Purchase from France, effectively doubling the size of the US with the stroke of a pen. In economic policy, Adams was a Federalist from the Northeast of the U.S. who tended to favor commercial interests, and he presided over the passage of new taxes. By contrast, Jefferson was a Republican and espoused a vision of an agrarian America. Both Adams and Jefferson had been key figures in the American Revolution against England, but their military policies differed. Adams was continually wary of French (after The XYZ Affair) and British naval power, so he pushed to augment the American navy, but he saw the provisional army only as an emergency measure. Jefferson, by contrast, wanted all military spending to be limited and for the navy to be used only for defense. He ended up paying tribute to Barbary pirates in the Mediterranean rather than conduct a costly war overseas.

An original conclusion should consider a fresh perspective on how their tenures changed the American Presidency. These two men were close friends and both had been instrumental in politics during the Revolutionary War. In what ways were their presidencies true to their particular revolutionary beliefs? Jefferson and Adams were also two of the earliest presidents when the American presidency was taking shape. What new powers did they obtain for their successors? How did their actions shape America's future and the contours of future presidencies? You don't have to tackle all of these fascinating questions, but choose one of them to enhance your discussion.

> ➤ *QUICK TIP:*
> *THE FOUR HORSES OF HISTORY*

All categories of comparison in a History essay involve four major components:

1. The Economy (Agriculture vs. Industry; taxes, tariffs; trade; growth vs. decline).

2. Social/Cultural Change (new artistic advances, social movements, cases taken up by the Supreme Court).

3. Political Leadership (leaders and their coalitions, governing style, laws passed).

4. Foreign and Military Policies (pro-war or anti-war; imperialist vs. isolationist).

These categories represent the key factors historians use to evaluate a particular era or a particular leader. There might also be more specific categories within these broad ones. Political leadership could break down into Domestic vs. Foreign Policy. Because they can have sweeping effects politically and socially (and perhaps even economically), Supreme Court cases could be its own category of comparison. Begin with any three of these four big categories and feel free to be more specific, depending on the essay you want to write. You'll be able to structure an excellent compare and contrast essay.

The Change Over Time Essay

Stories grip us because they portray characters who change over time. These changes can be slow and gradual, or sudden. Either way, the story advances because things change, decisions are made, challenges are met, consequences faced, and the protagonists end up somewhere that is different from where they began. Taking stock of the beginning, middle, and end of a story gives you the perfect set-up for this essay structure.

Let's use another of Shakespeare's masterpieces that often appears on high school curricula: "**How** and **why** does Macbeth go from being a loyal soldier to a murderous ruler?" In this essay, you're looking at the progression of Macbeth's ambition and you're focusing on those moments in the story that lead him ever further down a brutal path.

1. What is Macbeth like in the beginning of the play (loyal, good warrior, honest thane)?

2. What is Macbeth like in the middle (ideas of grandeur are provoked by the witches and by his wife)?

3. What is he like at the end (forced to commit heinous acts to keep power as he arguably goes mad)?

There are many different arrows in your quiver for this essay. There's the murder of King Duncan early in the play. There's the murder of Banquo towards the middle. There's the order to kill Macduff's wife and children near the end. You don't have to mention these examples specifically, but you must chart Macbeth's murderous progression. Each paragraph in this essay should quote amply from the text—that's how you'll prove that your impression of Macbeth at each stage of his evolution is correct. Be careful not to move too quickly through these paragraphs. You'll really want to dwell on the changing character of Macbeth at each stage. What does he himself express about his decisions? What do other characters say about him, or to him, that influences his character? Your deciphering of Shakespeare's complicated language will be crucial to showing your teacher that you've read the play actively and with full attention to detail.

But even with all your excellent examples, taking aim at a clear thesis and an original conclusion can be tricky. You'll want to consult your notes and really brainstorm to tease out your *personal* reactions to Macbeth's journey. Why does this happen to him? Because of his ambition for power. What excites his ambition? The witches, Lady Macbeth, his own idea of himself as king. To what extent, then, is Macbeth a hero or a villain? Where is Shakespeare in all this? What is he trying to say about unbridled lust for power?

> **➤ SUMMING UP**
>
> **Goldilocks**, **Compare And Contrast**, and **Change Over Time** formats provide the essential structures for essays because they organize your argument in a way that makes it both clear and provable. So before you write, think about which kind of essay structure best suits your argument. Knowing *in advance* what structure you'll use will save you time because it will help shape your evidence into organized sections and provide a logical flow of thought for the reader.

Bad Essay Structures

And now the bad (which can also get ugly).

The Emperor's New Clothes Essay

The structure of **The Emperor's New Clothes** bad essay borrows its name from the Hans Christian Anderson fairy tale about an Emperor who wants to look so fancy and fashionable that he hires two weavers to make him a set of clothes from a special fabric they claim will be invisible to anyone who is stupid. The two weavers finish the suit and dress the Emperor, who then parades before his subjects wearing the "invisible fabric." It takes only a child to realize that it's the Emperor who's stupid. He isn't wearing any clothes at all; he's walking around completely naked.

An Emperor's New Clothes Essay has no worthwhile content and is an attempt to fool the teacher with fancy frills. Students who write this sort of essay usually have good vocabularies (or they overuse the thesaurus button), but they are intellectually lazy. Fancy words, hyperbolic claims, and, in some cases, slick argumentation fail to hide the truth that nothing important is actually being said. Underneath it all, the essay is naked.

Here's an outstanding example of a naked essay introduction that displays some key elements of bad writing:

"In William Shakespeare's world-famous tragedy, *Hamlet,* the young monarch of Elsinore embarks upon a savage revenge-quest of epic proportions. For the prince of Denmark, white-hot rage over his father's death has prompted his epic quest for revenge. He seeks to destroy all in his path who prevent him from achieving his righteous revenge. He has to learn to be a man and, in the process, he acts murderously in order to avenge his father's death."

Look at the horrible **colloquialisms**: "of epic proportions," "to destroy all in his path," "learn to be a man." They're vague expressions that generalize Hamlet's journey instead of pointing to the specifics that make the plot exciting. They're so full of bluster and trumped-up melodrama that they don't get at the heart of Hamlet's quest at all.

The **overwriting** and **hyperbole** lead to useless generality ("world-famous" and "epic") and **vagueness** ("young monarch" and "acts murderously") and an over-the-top approach ("savage," "white-hot rage," "righteous revenge") that isn't part of formal essay writing. The words may be somewhat fancy, but they obscure any potential clarity or analysis of the ideas underneath and they get in the way of your own personal response to the material.

What's clear from this Emperor's New Clothes sample intro is that the writer has—maybe—one idea: that Hamlet is angry and wants revenge. No amount of fancy words or repetition can hide the absence of both any development of this too-obvious generality and any intention to provide specific examples as proof. It is clear that the writer has nothing interesting to say.

➢ *SUMMING UP*

Don't dress up a naked essay with fancy words and phrases! You might think you're putting one over the teacher, but you'll get a bad grade when you reveal there is no content to your "invisible fabric."

The Frankenstein Essay

The Frankenstein Essay gets its name from Mary Shelley's novel about a science experiment gone wrong. A scientist, Victor Frankenstein, manages to breathe life into a creature made of human limbs and organs taken from corpses. The creature ("It's alive! It's alive!") has a difficult existence because its parts aren't very well integrated (not to mention that everyone in the world outside Dr. Frankenstein's laboratory thinks it's hideous). At the end of the book, the monstrous creation turns on its creator and murders many of Frankenstein's family and friends.

Frankenstein Essays turn on their creators because the writer hasn't found a way to fit all his or her ideas into one argument. The leg is one idea, the arm is another; the heart beats quickly, the head thinks slowly. It's all out of whack because ideas unrelated to each other have been jammed together. The monster is trying to live, to feel, to think, to communicate, but its body parts are working at cross-purposes. (It can barely stand because its legs are of unequal length.)

Here's a sample Frankenstein body paragraph about the period in American History from 1865 to 1890:

"After the Civil War, America had to put itself back together again. Northern plans for Reconstruction took many different forms. There was Andrew Johnson's failed attempt, followed by that of the Radical Republicans, who wanted harsh terms placed on the South before they were allowed to rejoin the Union. Newly freed black slaves began to migrate to Northern cities, which left the Southern economy in desperate need of labor. Because no land was distributed to freed slaves or poor whites, the sharecropping system developed, which entrenched poor farmers in cycles of debt. The presidency of Ulysses S. Grant was also clouded with controversy and scandal. Grant was a drunk and presided over the end of Northern military rule in the South. Meanwhile, industrialization, especially in the North, began to drive America towards the Gilded Age, in which wealthy oil, steel, and railroad tycoons made huge profits at the expense of their workers, who labored for low wages and in poor conditions."

A body paragraph like this is a monstrous creation. It begins by talking about Reconstruction, then transitions abruptly into the experience of freed slaves after the Civil War, then touches on Grant's presidency, and finally ends with the Gilded Age. **Each of those topics should be its own essay.** Though the writer provides details, and though the writing is acceptable, the paragraph breezes along without developing one specific idea. Yes, poor blacks and whites fell victim to sharecropping. Yes, workers did labor in factories under poor and unsafe conditions. Yes, robber barons did make tons of money by taking advantage of workers, and, yes, Reconstruction did go through several failed stages. All true, but: the pieces don't fit together!

> ➤ *SUMMING UP*

You want the bones, flesh, and blood of your essay to belong to the same creature. If you find yourself writing three different essays in the same paper, you must amputate an arm or a leg and, by cutting away, save your essay from its own monstrosity—lest it (and your teacher) turn on you!

The Lemming Essay

The final bad essay structure, **The Lemming Essay**, is taken from those furry creatures who, as it is proverbially said, following each other in a line, will relentlessly march over a cliff and plummet to their deaths. Lemmings are cute and fuzzy, but aren't all that discerning. Watching them march over the cliff, you just want to shout: "Wake up! Look at what you're about to do!" In other words, lemmings must be saved from themselves.

A Lemming Essay endlessly repeats the same, vague, unchallenging idea with no attempt to find something original, personal, or engaging. Take a look at a sample Lemming conclusion:

"In *Pride and Prejudice*, Jane Austen portrays Elizabeth Bennet as someone who has trouble finding a husband. Elizabeth entertains many husband options, but she cannot find one that seems to fit. The social constraints on women in Britain in the 1800s left many women in the same position. They were forced to wait for a suitable husband to come along. Elizabeth is somewhat fickle in determining whom she wants to marry. She makes mistakes in judging potential husbands. Eventually, she marries Darcy. Austen shows how at first Elizabeth cannot find a good fit for a husband, but in the end, Elizabeth finds a good match in Darcy."

Wake up! You're about to lead the reader right over the edge. This atrocious conclusion contains a hallmark of bad writing: unnecessary **repetition**. The entire paragraph could be condensed into one or two sentences, following which more compelling questions could be asked and answered that would reveal a personal perspective on Elizabeth's choices. How does her judgment change over time? What does she learn along the way, and what might Jane Austen therefore be saying about the process of finding a good match among the lesser aristocracy in 19th century England? You're right: Elizabeth is fickle, and she has difficulty finding love. So what? That thought alone won't save you as your essay marches over the edge of the cliff and plummets to its death.

> ➤ *SUMMING UP*
>
> You cannot simply keep repeating your (one) idea. It will lead your teacher, who has to grade not only your paper, but also those of your classmates, to want to leap off a cliff. Wake up!

CHAPTER 4

Poetry

For many high schoolers, the word "Poetry" is fraught with ominous associations. For some, it means complete confusion; for others, it is a snoozefest. Like it or not, however, at some point in high school you'll take a poetry class and you will have to find ways to engage with the poems and make them meaningful to you. We can hope that you will discover that poetry is more than just overblown language—some of which rhymes and, yes, can be difficult to understand.

Let it be said that without a good teacher, poetry is in fact boring and/or overwhelming. Good teachers will combat the poetry malaise* by bringing poems to life: reading them out loud, calling attention to the rhythm of the verse or the poet's choice of words, inspiring students to respond personally to the perspective of the poet.

* *malaise, noun* — from the French, "malaise," meaning "sickness." It means a weariness and weakening of effort.

Bad teachers merely make students memorize lists of technical terms: alliteration, assonance, iambic pentameter, rhyme scheme, enjambment, simile, metaphor, and so on. All of these terms are important, but they're meaningless if you don't know *why* they're important: they are devices or techniques that help the poet express himself. So what, then, is the poet trying to say by using such devices? That's your job to figure out.

> ➤ *QUICK TIP:*
> *A POEM IS NOT JUST A POEM*

Poems come in so many different forms and styles that it's hard to make any absolute points about the range of poems you're likely to encounter. I encourage my students to give up on the word "poetry" and instead think of each poem as a piece of art from a different or related genre: a song, a diary entry, a short film, a painting, a shopping list, a tweet, and so on. Thinking of a poem as a painting opens your reading to the vibrant images within the words. Likewise, if you read a poem aloud, you might hear how much it sounds like a jazz standard or like a showtune or like rap. Some poems are deeply confessional, revealing thoughts and feelings as if from a private diary. So keep in mind that a poem is not just a poem: place it in a different form to help bring the words to life.

Crucial to an essay about poetry is that you must change what you mean by "proving an argument." Poetry doesn't quite work that way. History is full of facts, dates, causes, results. Long fiction has a fully realized plot, characters, and relationships to develop. Poetry, however, is not data. It's about experience, mystery, memory, allusion, feelings, self-expression. Yes, the poet probably had a point in writing, something that made her pick up a pen instead of picking up a paintbrush. But it's really your task to delve into the words (what is written and what may be hiding behind what is written) and come up with what is resonant for you. Because poetry is personal, be prepared to throw away strict conceptions of "right" and "wrong" and, instead, find what meaningful, personal reactions the poem evokes in you.

➤ SUMMING UP

A good poetry class will help bring poems to life. To appreciate a poem on your own, think of a poem as a song, a painting, a series of moving images. It will enable you to demystify it and make it more vibrant—to make it more than just confusing words on a page. Poetry is a personal experience, and thus has no rights or wrongs.

Formal and Informal Poetry

Poetry falls into two categories: **Formal** and **Informal**.

Formal Poetry

The **formal poetry** you are likely to read consists mostly of sonnets by Shakespeare and Wordsworth (maybe also by Donne, Keats, Yeats, Whitman, Shelley). Sonnets are sometimes difficult to appreciate because they have "rules" that require the compression of the poet's thoughts into distinct lines (three "quatrains" of four lines each, followed by one "couplet" consisting of two lines). Sonnets also have a special rhyming pattern within each quatrain and couplet. Sounds tricky? Well, the sonnet form itself is actually an excellent guide to unpacking the author's meaning because she has arranged her thoughts in such an organized way!

Sonnets present a reliable form that mirrors the **Five-Paragraph Essay**, and sonnets, like the analytical essays discussed earlier, have central arguments that require example-based evidence. The first quatrain introduces the subject or topic on which the poem will elaborate (the intro/thesis paragraph). The second quatrain builds upon the topic by shaping the argument further (providing more evidence through new examples). The third quatrain furthers the argument (by offering another example). Then the couplet puts a nice twist on the whole discussion and wraps up the sonnet with a ribbon (conclusion).

As you read a sonnet, pay attention to how the changing perspective of the speaker finds its way from the first quatrain to the couplet, how he expresses his feelings about love, nature, you-name-it. When you discuss a sonnet, you must track that argument.

Here is Shakespeare's Sonnet 18, *Shall I Compare Thee To A Summer's Day?*

Shall I compare thee to a summer's day?
Thou art more lovely and more temperate.
Rough winds do shake the darling buds of May,
And summer's lease hath all too short a date.

Sometime too hot the eye of heaven shines,
And often is his gold complexion dimmed;
And every fair from fair sometime declines,
By chance, or nature's changing course, untrimmed;

But thy eternal summer shall not fade,
Nor lose possession of that fair thou ow'st,
Nor shall death brag thou wand'rest in his shade,
When in eternal lines to Time thou grow'st.

So long as men can breathe, or eyes can see,
So long lives this, and this gives life to thee.

The speaker here is comparing the woman he loves to a summer day. The argument proceeds as follows:

First quatrain:
Intro/thesis

Is it possible to compare you to a day in summer?
Yes, let me try it.
You're cooler than a summer day.
Nature can be violent and windy.
Summer ends on September 21.

Second quatrain:
First body paragraph with examples as evidence

Besides, the summer sun can really be sweltering.
And clouds can block it, too.
Not to mention, flowers grow, but also die
As the seasons change.

Third quatrain:
Second body paragraph with new evidence

But you're beautiful all the time.
And you'll never lose that special glow you have.
And you'll never die
Because I wrote a poem about you that will make you
live forever.

Couplet:
Conclusion

As long as men are alive
So will this poem be read, which means you'll also be
alive for a really long time

Of course, my essential argument-paraphrase lacks any appreciation of Shakespeare's poetic language. It's just the facts; it's what the poem is saying, more or less. But that clear understanding of the construction of the argument is essential to its analysis.

Now, to this analysis you must add your own awareness and appreciation of the pictures the poem is presenting through the poet's choice of words. In Sonnet 18, Shakespeare provides particular and exquisite images of nature. In the first quatrain the wind is shaking the blossoms of a flower ("the darling buds of May"). The second quatrain offers us the clouds passing in front of the sun ("his gold complexion dimmed"). In the third quatrain is an image of a dead soul crossing into the underworld ("nor shall death brag thou wand'rest in his shade").

These pictures add up to what is meant when your teacher asks you to comment on the **imagery** in the poem. We can all see that Shakespeare is making a comparison between summer and his lover, but *how* does he do it? By presenting striking images of nature that add depth and drama to his central argument.

The strong imagery of Sonnet 18 is what makes me appreciate it as more than just a "poem." To me, it's a painting. That's how vivid the images of nature are. I see an oil-on-canvas painting of a hot summer sun baking the fields and a watercolor of thunderstorm winds bearing down on wildflowers. Considered this way, Sonnet 18 is no longer just words on a page; it has come to life.

Now, and most important, how do *you* respond to those images? To my ear and eye, Shakespeare makes nature seem awesome. He describes the sun as the "eye of heaven." I never thought of it that way! And it has a "gold complexion," as does, perhaps, someone's face. That technique is called **personification** (giving human qualities to inanimate objects). If the speaker's lover is more beautiful than something with golden skin tones, she must be pretty stunning! In fact, she herself is like a force of nature—one so "lovely," "temperate," and "fair" that even nature's mightiest forces cannot equal her. "Summer's lease" (that is, summertime) "hath all too short a date"—it ends after three months. But the speaker's lover will live on in "eternal lines to Time." It's quite a romantic and hyperbolic idea.

But you might have a different reaction. You might think it's unhealthy for ol' Billy Shakes to have fallen so hard for this woman. Or that he's bragging, that he's actually praising his own poetry more than this woman; he does say that it is the *poem* that will live forever and therefore enable his love to live forever. There's probably an interesting essay about whether beauty can continue to exist through words after it has disappeared from the flesh—what a great and original perspective for a conclusion! However *you* respond, whatever *your* thoughts are, that's what matters.

Your teacher will also want you to point out other formal aspects of a sonnet:

Rhyme scheme, the end-of-line rhyming pattern that helps unify the poem and gives the form its signature sounds, in this case ABAB CDCD EFEF GG. In Sonnet 18, the words that end each line are as follows:

"day" (A)
"temperate" (B)
"may" (A)
"date" (B)

"shines" (C)
"dimmed" (D)
"declines" (C)
"untrimmed" (D)

And so on;

Alliteration and **Assonance**, the awareness of the repetition of sounds (consonants and vowels, respectively) in particular words and phrases, such as "*ch*ance... *ch*anging" and "l*i*nes to T*i*me";

Simile and **Metaphor**, the comparison of a specific person, object, or situation to something loftier, more abstract, more imaginative—in this case that a person can be like a "summer day." Similes are further distinguishable because they make the comparison using the words "like" or "as." A metaphor might only contain an implied comparison, as in Shakespeare's famous phrase "All the world's a stage";

Iambic pentameter, the "standard" meter of English verse that consists of one unstressed, then one stressed syllable, five times per line (as seen in almost every line of the poem!). Iambs are like heartbeats because the rhythm of the unstressed-stressed combination sounds like the lub-DUB of a heart beating: lub-DUB, lub-DUB, lub-DUB, lub-DUB, lub-DUB. Where do you think the expression "to learn by heart" comes from? Why, from Shakespeare. To "learn by heart" originally meant to memorize iambic pentameter. That's how crucial the iamb is to the natural rhythm of English.

Take care not to write an essay that merely lists poetic devices. It's good that you've noticed them in the poem, but your essay should aim to make a point about what the poem is trying to express and then use the poetic devices *in support of* that claim. One body paragraph should not be organized around how many examples of alliteration you've found. The body paragraph should speak to a particular thematic or emotional aspect of the poem, for which the sounds the poet chooses to alliterate can be excellent evidence.

➤ SUMMING UP

The formal poetry you're most likely to encounter will consist of sonnets. These poems have a distinct form that mirrors the five-paragraph essay in terms of argumentation: intro/thesis (first quatrain), first body paragraph (second quatrain), second body paragraph (third quatrain), conclusion (couplet). Sonnets obligate you to follow the argument as it evolves and to pay attention to important technical devices. As always, what matters is your personal reaction. After you analyze, what sounds/images does the poem offer up to you? How do you react to the speaker's argument and to the presented images? What does the poem make you feel?

Informal Poetry

Unlike sonnets, **informal poetry** has no immediately recognizable or even consistent structure. Informal poetry is often called **free verse** (no rhyme scheme and no specific meter). Have you ever read a poem by E.E. Cummings? The words are arranged on the page almost willy-nilly. (Or are they?)

The big question on your mind as you read a work of informal poetry should be: **How does the form of the poem express its content?**

Form refers to the technical elements just discussed above (rhyme scheme, imagery, iambic pentameter), but also the "picture" the words make on the page—the shape of the text—as well as its sound when read aloud. How long, how short, is each line? Are the thoughts complete at the end of a line or do they continue to the next? Do the words flow in a kind of rhythm? If so, are they fast-paced or slow? Do the words rhyme at the end of the line or within the line? What is the descriptive imagery: birds? flowers? water? fire? These are all formal elements of a poem—how it looks on the page and how it sounds when spoken.

Content refers to the subject, or subjects, of the poem—what it is about. Does it describe a happy time in the summer? A sad, quiet moment? Is it a love poem? Is the poet remembering his happy childhood, or is he conveying fear and confusion at growing up? Or is it about a bug? Subjects can be endless.

Good poets use formal techniques to bring out the content of their ideas. If the poet is describing flying over the surface of the ocean in a sailboat, then the words, too, should seem to fly across the page. That's how the poet captures the experience of sailing. If the poet is facing deep loneliness, then the words, too, will seem isolated, detached, set apart. Look for these connections between form and content to reveal what the poet is trying to express.

➤ *QUICK TIP:*
READ THREE TIMES

Having trouble getting the sights and sounds of the poem? Try reading it three times. Poems are usually short, so this is not such a difficult task. Why three? Because good poets pack their poems with details that take time to discover and to appreciate fully.   T h e first time through, just read with **curiosity**. Let it bounce along easily, and don't be too concerned with catching everything. What's important is your openness to the world of the poem and your wonder at the poet's words. At the end, maybe you will have an inkling as to what the poem is about. Jot that down at the top of the page.

The second time through, read the poem **out loud**. You're trying to get your ear involved, to hear rhymes that you may have missed the first time, or groups of sounds that are repeated or that are particularly evocative. Maybe you missed a great turn of phrase, or a striking image. Speaking the words aloud will prompt your imagination to think of the poem as a piece of music and to create visual images; imagery and music cannot be picked up just with the eye. Reading the poem a second time, circle the images and sounds that have now come alive. At the top of the page, add new thoughts to your notes about the poem as a whole. How do you *now* understand what the poet may be driving at?

The third time through, read **line by line**. In other words, don't let the text flow smoothly from line to line. Instead, make yourself pause at the end of each line before going on to the next. Like bricks becoming a house, the lines are what the poet uses to build the shape of the verse. Going line by line will help you see where the bricks are short or long, sturdy or flimsy, connected to the rest of the house or forced to stand alone. After reading it three times, go to the top of your page and refine what you think the poem is about. Edit that initial idea so it expresses more completely the situation or perspective the poem describes.

A great example of the union of form and content is Elizabeth Bishop's "The Fish." Here's a small snippet:

> He was speckled with barnacles,
> fine rosettes of lime,
> and infested
> with tiny white sea-lice,
> and underneath two or three
> rags of green weed hung down.
> While his gills were breathing in
> the terrible oxygen
> —the frightening gills,
> fresh and crisp with blood,
> that can cut so badly—
> I thought of the coarse white flesh
> packed in like feather,
> the big bones and the little bones,
> the dramatic reds and blacks
> of his shiny entrails,
> and the pink swim-bladder
> like a big peony.

Let's **read the poem three times**:

Reading these lines the first time through, I am caught by the drama of the scene. I can write at the top of the page: "Someone is inspecting a strange fish that he/she has just caught."

I read it again out loud. I hear the **assonance** of "tiny white sea-lice" and "green weed." There's also a subtle, end-line rhyme: "breathing in" and "oxygen." My ear also picks up some descriptive language. The oxygen is described as being "terrible" and the gills are called "frightening." Reading out loud has helped me discover the fish through the poet's use of descriptive words. We discover the body of the fish as the fisherman discovers it. I have a strong image of a fish flopping around in someone's hands.

I read it a third time, going line by line. Forcing myself to slow down, I feel the impact of the words at the ends of the lines. Words like "barnacles" and "sea-lice." I had missed that the word "three" at the end of the line helps to accentuate the rhyme in "green weed" on the next line. That "ee" sound is really piercing; it shrieks at me. I can now see those "gills," covered in "blood" because of the "terrible oxygen" that is preventing the fish from breathing. I had missed the "coarse white flesh" and the anatomy of the fish, with its "big bones" and "little bones." All these things now come alive for me as I pause at the end of each line to let the images appear fully. I'm also struck by how much color Bishop includes: lime, white, green, white, red, black, pink. Twice, she describes the fish's body in terms of flowers: rosettes and peonies.

Now that I've read the poem three times, I can go back and revise my initial idea: "In fascinating and somewhat gruesome detail, Bishop describes the beautiful and battered anatomy of a freshly caught old fish. A fisherman notices the fish's strange shapes and vivid colors." This revision now represents what I think is the **content** of the poem, which leads to the obvious question: how does the form of the poem express its content?

Take a look at the shape of the poem on the page. What do you see? Bishop could have written the whole poem on one or two lines or in one paragraph, but she didn't. She chose to divide the thoughts into various small and large chunks, kind of like the "big bones and the little bones" of the fish itself. For me, taking note of the shape of the words on the page is evocative of the experience of inspecting a strange fish in one's hands.

As the reader, I inspect the words in the same way: there are short lines and there are long lines. Look at how the words are packed onto the page, much like the "coarse white flesh" of the fish. Look at how abnormally the end-lines rhyme and how powerfully the middle-lines rhyme. It's as if the poem is just speckled with rhyme, much like the fish's flesh is speckled with barnacles. The image of the gills is particularly striking. Gills are vertical slits on the side of a fish through which fish breathe. Turn the paper to the side: the lines look like the fish's gills with white space, the "terrible oxygen," circulating around them. The white space helps us appreciate the black letters on the page, but for a fish, this kind of breathing is deadly. The varying lengths of the lines now seem to represent the fish's struggle to breathe. Some breaths are shallow, others are deep.

I could go on. The rest of the poem offers more examples of how the shape of the words on the page evokes the shape of the fish in the fisherman's hands. But enough has already been noted to make an argument: "In Elizabeth Bishop's 'The Fish,' the poet's attention to the dynamic shape of the words on the page suggests the anatomy of this strange and wonderful freshly caught fish. The fish is struggling to live, just as the poet herself makes the words come alive for the reader by placing them on the page in specific ways."

One final thought here. Turning the paper again to the side, I get a very different image. The varying lengths of the lines now look to me like the waves of the ocean. Some are high and seem to be crashing down. Others are low, bottomed out. The shifting surface of the lines is like the shifting surface of water. The poem is perhaps not only about a beautiful, old, battered fish, but also about the person who has caught it. The shape of the words on the page now suggests to me the shifting lives of these *two* creatures, fisherman and fish—lives that are spent, heroically and tragically, on the huge ocean. What a nice, original idea for a conclusion.

➢ **SUMMING UP**

Informal poetry requires you to answer a central question: how does the form of the poem express its content? Form refers to technical, visual, and aural aspects of the poem when seen on the page and read out loud. Content is the material the poet is trying to bring to life. As always, your personal reactions will make all the difference when it comes to writing an original essay.

Developing good writing skills takes time—in fact, it takes a lifetime. Some students are born with great instincts about how to structure arguments; some are wonderfully creative writers who feel hemmed in by essay structure. One thing I know for sure is that if you commit yourself to the writing process, your effort *will* yield results. This will take time. Don't expect that B- to become an A overnight.

I insist that anything you write can always be made better. That means that, even after macro- and micro-editing, even after your teacher reads it and asks for a revision (if you're lucky), your writing can always be improved. How it can be improved depends on what you're trying to say. Perhaps a tricky argument has required you to use lots of quotations from the text. In reading over your essay, you might find that the argument is lost among so many—perhaps too many—examples. Try deleting one to let the argument breathe more freely. Or, if you find that your case might be too flimsy, strengthen it with another example. Professional writers obsess over individual words—whether to say "the" or "a"—as much as they struggle with whether the hero should live or die. So always be prepared to make your essay better.

Finally, expect your writing style to change over time. You will develop ways of expressing yourself that you really like. You'll find other ways clunky or heavy or breezy or abstruse. You will read someone else's essay and have critical thoughts about your fellow student's writing. That's all good! It means that writing has taken up residence within you and that you have achieved the main goal of writing: intelligent self-expression through words. Writing will have become a creative, useable, enjoyable personal resource for you, and you will come to write things that, in Shakespeare's words, will with a little luck grow "in eternal lines to Time."

ACKNOWLEDGMENTS

I have been blessed to have had wonderful teachers in my life, all of whom have contributed to the way I write, to the way I engage with language, literature, history and art, and to the way I see the world. Without them, this book could never have been born. In particular, I gratefully acknowledge the inspiring teaching of Dr. Stephanie Russell and Dr. Adam Bresnick.

I also wish to thank the students I have taught over the years. As I taught, so did I learn from you all. Your questions made me teach better and challenged me to come up with new and exciting ways of getting to the heart of a History lesson or of a challenging poem. Again, without you, this book would not exist.

Joe Spieler—agent, editor, actor, mensch—deserves special appreciation for his time, encouragement, and worthy criticisms. I owe Michael Howard—writer, actor, teacher—a debt of gratitude for showing me that there is always something deeper to unearth within a piece of literature—a truth both personal and universal waiting to astonish us.

To my parents, Stuart Liebman and Lois Greenfield, who always wanted to know what I thought, and who encouraged those ideas, whatever they were; who fostered an appreciation of literature, history, and art in all its forms; who stayed up late helping me with revisions; who always want to read what I write.

I gratefully acknowledge the insight, support, and encouragement of friends and colleagues, in particular:

Iris Blasi, Jeff Vinikoor, Andrew Fippinger, Alexis Rubin, and Elisabeth Gray.

Finally, to my wife, Kimiye, who tolerated my long hours of writing and editing and pushed me to bring this book to fulfillment.

Without all of you, there would be no book.

About The Author

Jesse Liebman was born, raised, and lives in New York City. He attended the Columbia Grammar School, then the Collegiate School, from which he graduated in 1999. He majored in Classics at Princeton (Summa Cum Laude, induction into the Phi Beta Kappa Society), was Salutatorian of the class of 2003, and was awarded the Samuel D. Atkins prize for the best Senior Thesis in the Classics Department.

Jesse began tutoring in 2004 and has worked with students from the five boroughs of New York in disciplines including: Writing, English, History, Latin, Greek, French, the SAT (Verbal and Math), and numerous other SAT II tests and AP exams. He has also studied acting with such luminaries as Mike Nichols and George Morrison at The New Actors Workshop and with Michael Howard in his private master class.

Made in the USA
Monee, IL
27 December 2020

55657984R10069